The Challenge of the City

A Biblical View

Stuart Murray

Sovereign World Ltd
PO Box 777
Tonbridge
Kent TN11 9XT
England

ISBN: 1 85240 113 3

Typeset by CRB (Drayton) Typesetting Services, Drayton, Norwich
Printed in England by Clays Ltd, St Ives plc.

To Neil and Robert

Contents

Foreword

Stuart Murray has written a fascinating and remarkable study based on the theme of the city throughout the Bible. Moreover his book is a manual for every Christian who wants to learn the nature and the character of the city in which they live and it is a literal goldmine of guidance for all believers called to take their city for God.

From its beginnings, Stuart points out, every city is created with a life of its own, a corporate personality with a culture, and a distinctive personality. The city also becomes a 'power' and the powers have always striven for mastery. For example, the first nations of the ancient world were city-states, and the mightiest cities became the ancient empires of world powers, like Rome or Babylon or Assyria. All these same things have now grown to gigantic stature, because we live in the day of the mega city and the day of the superpower.

In the Fall the city also symbolises man's corporate rebellion against God; it becomes idolatrous and its idolatry leads to demonisation. Satan has established his ruling demonic powers to control and dominate the structures of the city, bringing confusion and chaos into any attempts to diagnose its problems and hardening the city's resistance to change.

But even in the darkness of the city I catch Stuart's passion for its hope, because he realises that the Bible reveals it is not a lost cause. It is where the Holy Spirit comes at Pentecost and where the Church's mission begins. They will be judged by God for their sinfulness, but the cities are also the object of redemption and part of the 'all things' of reconciliation. In the age to come, they will be under the headship of Christ and they will be an arena for the Father's glory!

In the third section, 'Strategies for the City' Stuart's heart beats like Psalm 137:4–6,

> *'If I forget you, O Jerusalem . . . if I do not remember you, if I do not consider Jerusalem my greatest joy.'*

He speaks not just out of this vision but out of hard won experience. What does it mean to pray for the city and confess its sin? We need to realise like Nehemiah that the city is corporately guilty but that we also share in that corporate guilt. What does it mean to seek the peace of the city or to bring the prophetic word of God to the city, or how can you empower the powerless in the city?

Just as importantly we have to face the realism of mission in the modern city. We need to hear from those who live there how the language of salvation can be communicated to our increasingly multi-racial cities.

This book shows us new ways of church planting and evangelising the men and women, boys and girls of the inner city. Above all it demonstrates how in worship, prayer and praise, deliverence, power and healing, the Body of Christ has its own life and its modern authenticity.

I believe this great book describes the characteristics of multitudes of unknown churches in many cities of poverty, but it will also be the means of seeding many more to begin.

Tom Marshall
Sydney
Australia

PART I

Introducing the City

Chapter 1

Welcome to the City

'Don't waste your time in the East End. Nothing has ever happened there and nothing ever will.'

Not the most encouraging message for a young man about to move to the East End of London as a member of a small mission team! The speaker was an elderly Christian man who had lived for the past twenty years on the outskirts of London. Although the East End was only twenty minutes away by car, for him (as for many others in this affluent suburb) it was a different world, an ungodly place where decent people were not to be found, where Christians had no need to venture. His advice was crystal clear. To him it was as self-evident as the answer to a question posed long ago by another sceptic: *'Can anything good come out of Nazareth?'*[1] – and just as wrong.

My instinctive reaction was that this comment was a denial of the power of God and the justice of God. Either God finds the inner cities too tough to deal with or else He prefers to spend His time in the suburbs where most Christians live. I could find no way of squaring this with the biblical emphasis on God's commitment to the poor nor with the ministry of Jesus. It seemed to me that the inner city was just the sort of place where Jesus would have 'wasted' His time. But I have since discovered that this negative view of urban mission is common among Christians.

I spent twelve years 'wasting my time' in East London. There were times when life was tough. I was threatened, physically attacked, burgled on several occasions, and shared the pain of others as they faced similar pressures. Money was always in short supply, especially during the first six years when I had no fixed income but experienced all the excitement and insecurity of 'living by faith'. Being homeless with a young family for a few weeks was not easy. Was my friend right? Was I just banging my head against a brick wall?

Five months after moving into East London I started to meet each Sunday morning with five others (including my wife Rachel, to whom I was then engaged). From this group a church gradually developed. It grew in various ways – through conversions, through Christians moving into the area, and through a merger with another local fellowship. When I left the area in 1989, it had some 230 adult members and about 80 children, a mixture of born and bred East Londoners and those with roots elsewhere, drawn from over twenty nationalities. We were involved in specialist ministries among the local Asian and African communities, and we had developed a Christian school. The nature of the area is such that there had been several hundred others who had been converted through the ministry of the church or in membership at various times, but who had then moved away.

This growth was exciting but not without difficulties. The church had no premises of its own and had inexperienced leaders without formal training for ministry. The growth that took place was not the product of clever strategy or gifted leaders. It is evidence rather of the grace of God, His commitment to work in the inner city, and His willingness to use ordinary people. My colleague Nigel Wright once described us as 'the church that breaks all the rules'. According to church growth principles, this church should not exist. But exist it does, as do many other new and growing churches in places where for generations Christians have been saying, 'Nothing will ever happen there.'

I am convinced that the inner city is near the top of God's agenda as we reach the end of the twentieth century. By 'inner city' I mean areas within our major cities which are densely populated, poorly resourced and suffering deprivation of various kinds. Other terms sometimes used, such as urban priority areas; and other locations, such as overspill housing estates, share similar characteristics. In this book I will refer to these situations as the 'inner city' and distinguish them from the city centre where commercial and political power is exercised and from the suburbs. I believe that the Church needs to acknowledge and repent of its long neglect of these areas, and to mobilise its forces for a massive initiative of evangelism, church planting and compassionate ministry in the inner city.

Until fairly recently to say this would have produced little response. In the 1960s the few voices crying about the wilderness in our cities were largely ignored. In the West, Christians were moving out of cities and most mission agencies were still concentrating on overseas locations, rather than the mission field at home. Overseas mission was also mainly rural. But in the 1970s and 1980s things changed. To some extent we were forced to think about the inner city as the violence and frustration there erupted into our living rooms through the medium of television. Various reports and books were written by Christians. Some attempted to describe urban communities and to analyse the economic, physical, social and spiritual conditions in the inner city. Some were stories of church life and mission in the cities. Some were global in perspective and suggested strategies for action. Urban mission and ministry seemed to be rising up the Church's agenda. Funds were allocated, initiatives were taken, and in some circles the inner city seemed to be 'the flavour of the month'.

But by the early 1990s it was evident that more had been said than done, more planned than executed. In Britain a major survey revealed that during the past ten years inner city churches had lost members at three times the rate of suburban churches.[2] Furthermore, urban mission was starting to slip down the agenda again as the churches mistook words for action. Raising awareness, challenging misconceptions and providing accurate information were reasonable places to begin. But it was not enough to discuss the inner city, to produce reports and add seminars on urban mission to our conferences. A radical and lasting change of direction and a courageous strategy are needed if the Church of Jesus Christ is to capture the hearts and minds of urban people. Fine words must lead on to costly action.

The difficulties involved in urban mission are real and the

situation in the inner cities is often bleak, but negative attitudes towards the city and lack of involvement by the wider Church have helped to make the situation what it is. There is a vicious circle here which needs to be broken for the sake of the kingdom of God. If church growth and effective ministry are only possible in middle-class areas, what sort of God do we worship and of what value is the salvation we proclaim? The weakness of the Church in the inner city is an indictment on the Church as a whole.

The cities are crucial for the Church's mission, and it is the inner city areas that present the greatest challenge. But only a tiny percentage of our resources and personnel are invested here.[3] American missiologist Roger Greenway has written:

'Failure in winning the cities means failure in winning the world ... As the cities go, so go the nations. If winning the nations to Christ is our assignment, to the cities we must go. Yet, sadly we must confess that many of God's servants are in the same position as Jonah on the hillside, watching the city from a safe distance, and caring little whether it lives or dies.[4]

What will persuade Christians to become involved in urban mission? Stories about the inner city and church life there can play a part – not least by exposing the inaccuracy of the charge that 'nothing has ever happened there'. There are accounts available of great works of God in the inner city. In East London alone there have been significant moves of God which have resulted in many conversions and changes in social and economic conditions. The many Methodist churches and missions are reminders of John Wesley's preaching in the area. The statue of William Booth, the founder of the Salvation Army, a few yards from my first home in Tower Hamlets marks the spot where he began preaching in the open air. Nearby is the site of Tower Hamlets Mission founded by Frederick Charrington, a converted brewer, which in its heyday was packed with up to 5000 people and ministered to both social and spiritual needs. Similar stories could be told about inner city areas all over Europe and North America.[5]

There have been weaknesses, chief among them the failure to establish vibrant, indigenous, locally led churches. There has been an over-dependence on outside initiative and support and an inadequate concept of 'church'. But the stories do give lie to the idea that nothing has ever happened in the inner city.

I am not convinced, however, that stories are a sufficient foundation for the kind of urban strategy that is needed. I am grateful for the stories and would welcome more, but my aim here is different. For those who take the authority of the Bible seriously and who are prepared to have their attitudes and priorities governed by it, the crucial question is, 'what does the Bible say about the city?' Inner city areas are part of the city as a whole, so an understanding of the Bible's approach to the city is the starting point for urban mission. Such a major change of strategy and relocation of resources are required to reach the inner cities that only if we are persuaded that urban mission is a biblical priority will we be prepared to consider this upheaval. Without this foundation any remaining interest in or concern for the inner city will not effect a lasting change.

When we turn to the Bible we find that it is full of cities. There are at least 1400 references to cities from the early chapters of Genesis to the final chapter of Revelation. It is a major biblical theme. Most of the rest of this book will be given over to exploring these references and demonstrating that the widespread indifference or hostility towards the city still to be found among many Christians can only be maintained if a wealth of biblical data is ignored or completely misinterpreted.

At this point two questions may arise: 'hasn't such a study been made before?' and 'is such a study legitimate?'

Two fascinating and influential studies appeared a quarter of a century ago at a time when the Church was just beginning to think again about urban issues. Both used the city as a symbol of modern society rather than getting to grips with the nitty-gritty of urban life – as such neither provides an adequate basis for urban mission – and they reached very different conclusions. In 1965 Harvey Cox published *The Secular City*, which argued that the urbanisation of society and the secularisation that accompanies this are trends Christians should welcome, seeing them as a fulfilment of the biblical message. Five years later

Jacques Ellul published *The Meaning of the City*, which traces the theme of the city through the Bible and concludes that it is beyond salvation except by an act of God in establishing the New Jerusalem.

Neither book provides what is needed. *The Secular City* does not treat the biblical text seriously, reinterpreting it to fit in with preconceived philosophical ideas. Its assessment of the effects of urbanisation is naively optimistic and quite remote from urban realities. The implication is that the church has nothing distinctive to offer and no mission to peform.[6] *The Meaning of the City* is rooted in the Bible and, though some of its deductions are questionable, there is much that is useful here. But Ellul's view of the city is bleak and static. He calls his approach 'active pessimism', but he holds out no real hope that anything significant can be achieved in the cities of Earth before the return of Christ. I do not believe this approach does justice to the biblical material. My concern is to chart a course between unrealistic optimism and unjustified pessimism.

But is it legitimate to draw conclusions from the Bible about the shape of contemporary urban mission? Although there were cities in biblical times, some of them quite extensive, the vast majority lived in villages or small towns. Has the Bible anything to say to an urbanised world? We may argue that human nature has not changed so that the truths of the Bible apply to human beings in any environment. But does the Bible have any word for the cities and their millions of inhabitants? Or for the Church as it faces the urban challenge? Is there any point in asking what the Bible says about the city?

It has certainly been argued that it is not legitimate to 'move directly from biblical texts about cities to the modern phenomena of cities.'[7] Important biblical themes can be studied and applied to urban issues, but we are not to look for actual answers to urban problems in the stories of biblical cities. The Archbishop of Canterbury's Commission on Urban Priority Areas (ACUPA) states:

> 'It would be highly misleading if we were to propose a "theology of the city" that claimed to be appropriate to such a wide variety of situations.'[8]

15

A similar approach has been taken by several recent publications on the city.

I recognise the need for caution in applying texts and I agree that certain biblical themes (especially those relating to the poor, justice, the powers, shalom) are of great significance to urban mission, but I do believe there is a discernible 'theology of the city' in the Bible. Of course, if we are looking for guidance on social policies or architectural designs for cities of ten million people, we must look elsewhere or be content to draw conclusions from general principles – but then that is equally true for village planning. What the Bible does give us is insight into the meaning of the city, why it exists, what God thinks of it, its spiritual significance, its role in a fallen world, its influence on those who live in it or around it, how the Church is to approach it and what its future holds.

I am persuaded that the biblical vision of the city is clear and consistent. It faces squarely the evil and darkness of the city, but it is full of hope for the city and gives guidelines for effective urban ministry.

Raymond Bakke of Chicago tells of his encounter with some radical clergy:

> 'One liberal theologian argued that conservative evangelicals could not survive in the city. To take the Bible literally is to become anti-urban. God's favourite people were shepherds; his next favourite people were vine-growers and farmers; and his least favourite people were urban dwellers. This argument was important to me.'[9]

It is important to the cause of urban mission that this misconception of the biblical view of the city be dispelled – not by trying to evade what the Bible teaches, but by giving it the freedom to speak clearly and to challenge our ideas, fears and misgivings. Only then will we have a secure foundation to tackle the tremendous task of reaching our cities for Christ.

Chapter 2

Christians and the City

Before turning to the Bible, it is worth probing more deeply into the rather negative attitude towards the inner city that many Christians have. This attitude affects where we live, how we respond to information about the inner city, and how we understand the biblical material about cities. So in this chapter we will explore two issues: where in the city do Christians live? and why do they live where they do?

Doughnut Cities

A simple but memorable way to understand the situation in many Western cities is to meditate on a ring doughnut. There is the added benefit of being able to eat it once you have finished!

Most Christians live and worship in the suburban Bible belt that rings the city. In the middle there is a large hole where Christians are few and churches small. Christians from the suburbs may come into the centre of the city to work, but their homes, friends and churches are in the suburbs. Christians who move home tend to move away from the centre of the city rather than further in. Those who once lived in the inner city have moved out to the suburban ring; those already in the suburbs will either move to another suburb or further out still. There are exceptions to this rule, of course, and the redevelopment of some inner city areas may increase these exceptions, but the overall trend is very clear.

A more complex picture is provided by an archery target (see figure 1). The centre of the target (A) is the city centre, the

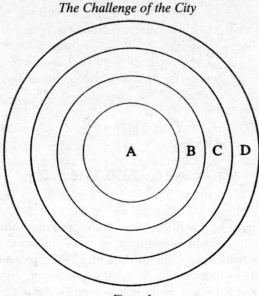

Figure 1

business and commercial area, the political and administrative hub. Relatively few people live in this area but huge numbers commute in to work each day. City-centre churches vary. Some are small and struggling and share the characteristics of those in the inner city. But quite a number are large and well-attended, boosted by students and professionals. Normally well-staffed and well-organised, they provide an important witness to Christ in the power centres of our cities. Several have developed effective and imaginative ministries towards the business community. These churches have much more in common with suburban churches than those in the inner city. They are middle-class in ethos and membership.

The third circle is the suburban ring (C). Although there are places where the church is weak, most suburbs have plenty of churches for the religious consumer to choose from. Many are prosperous and have excellent facilities, adequate staff and a large membership and budget. With many people moving into their pleasant neighbourhoods and settling there for many years, there are good prospects for steady growth and plenty of opportunities for ministry. In recent years many of these

18

churches have been enriched by charismatic renewal, which unlike Pentecostalism has so far been confined largely to white middle-class churches. Some suburban Christians not only commute to work but travel to church also, either into the city centre or to support struggling causes in the inner city.

Between the centre and the suburbs is a very different area, socially and spiritually, the inner city (B). There are still many imposing church buildings here but most of them are almost empty. Churches generally are small, weak, under-staffed, with either no facilities or huge unsuitable ones. There are fewer Christians here, in no small measure because of migration to the suburbs over many years. A significant number of Christians who do live here will not worship locally but travel to city-centre churches.

A few figures may help to illustrate the contrast between these zones. Churchgoing in most suburbs is around ten or twelve per cent of the population: it may be as high as fifteen per cent in some. Church leaders in the inner London Borough of Newham estimate the figure in their area to be two per cent. In Tower Hamlets it is probably as low as half of one per cent: a 1975 estimate of churchgoing in East London suggests 'only one person in every 200 attends a place of worship on Sunday.'[1] Some years ago Clifford Hill wrote:

'In the East End of London more than half the churches that existed in 1945 have now closed and if the present closure rate is maintained there will be no churches left at all by 1988.'[2]

We have passed this date and there are churches left but the warning remains. Similar statistics would document the same situation in North America and other European cities. Unless the Church wakes up to the disparity between the inner city and the suburbs, the doughnut picture will become ever more accurate.

The outer circle (D) is the area beyond the suburbs, rural areas and overspill housing estates which have much in common with the inner city. Here, too, in the villages and the housing estates, the churches tend to be weak and the Christians few. It is no part of my intention to suggest that the inner city is the only place where a redistribution of Christian resources is needed. I am aware that in many rural areas the Church is struggling to survive. And many of the large housing estates present a major challenge to Christian ministry.

I believe that this analysis is broadly true of most major Western cities, but I do not believe that this is God's best for the Church or His strategy for our cities. This concentration of Christians in the suburbs is not sensible. The criss-cross travelling of Christians every Sunday morning in our cities must look awfully foolish from heaven. In plain terms this means that many Christians are not living where they ought to be. I do not mean that they have disobeyed clear guidance about where they should live and worship, although this may be true of some, but that many have not been open to even consider certain areas. Cultural and material factors have ruled out certain options at the outset.

Attitudes to the City

Why do Christians live where they do? The fact that so many live in the suburbs shows that they value some aspects of the city – as a place of well-paid employment, entertainment, culture and material comfort. But how many have really thought through their identification with the suburban culture that is selfish, even parasitical? I know of no better summary of the suburban spirit than a statement contained in the official guide to a London suburb some years ago:

> 'Traditionally Woodford has always endeavoured to keep the disadvantages of civilisation at a proper distance without permitting the advantages to escape it.'

Can Christians in the suburbs sit easily with such sentiments? How serious is the unconscious cultural captivity of the suburban church?

But few Christians consider the alternative of living in the inner city and getting involved in God's mission to the city. Even those who have become concerned about the city are still sitting with Jonah on the hillside, even if they send a donation from time to time now. Why?

(1) Fear

Those who have little or no first-hand experience of inner city life are often fearful of such areas. Having watched numerous television reports on violence, crimes, riots and social problems they assume that inner cities are always like this. To live in such an area is something they would not contemplate, especially if there are children to be brought up.

(2) Hopelessness

Some are unwilling to be involved in urban mission because they fear failure and lack faith that anything can be accomplished. The East End of London has been nick-named, unfairly, 'the graveyard of evangelists'. Few church leaders will choose to move into the inner city. There is little prestige associated with such places and seemingly little prospect of building a thriving church. Many feel quite inadequate for the demands of such a ministry and are honest enough to say so.

(3) Confusion

Cities are complex rather than simple. The needs of urban people are often deep-rooted and very involved. Pastoral care is varied and demanding, and church-building requires a flexible approach rather than ready-made solutions. Urban mission often involves crossing barriers of race and class. For many Christians this is asking too much. The confusion they feel is partly the result of ignorance and distance; 'inner city Christians must interpret the city to their suburban brothers and sisters.'[3]

(4) Antagonism

Evidence submitted to ACUPA indicates that British antipathy to the city is especially strong and has a long history, reaching back to Roman times. Harvie Conn has documented a similar antipathy in the USA, where the 'American dream' is understood primarily as a rural or small-town vision.[4]

Consider a modern version of a familiar parable. A suburban Christian and an inner city Christian met at a convention and both started to pray. The suburban Christian used many fine phrases, thanking God for his pleasant home, his interesting and socially useful job, and the fine education his children were receiving. In particular today he was grateful that he did not have to live in the inner city where he would be surrounded by crime, stress and problems. He promised God that he would send a generous gift to an urban mission hall he knew of, and he prayed that his new friend would soon be able to move out into a nice suburban house. But the inner city Christian, who did not have many words, prayed: 'O God, help! Keep me faithful to you, and have mercy upon my city.'[5]

In spite of the renewed awareness of the inner city among the churches little will change until these attitudes of fear, hopelessness, confusion and antagonism are confronted. As long as the inner city is seen as a dirty, violent, crowded place with little to commend it, all the talk about urban mission will remain just talk. Many will continue to shelter behind the idea that all the talk about urban mission is unnecessary, trendy, and exaggerated.

I remember writing to the editor of a Christian magazine some time ago with a request that his magazine might from time to time deal with urban issues. Although the contents of the magazine were normally edifying, the articles were rather middle-class and not always appropriate to our local congregation. His response was that the principles taught in the magazine 'worked anywhere' and that all the talk around about urban areas was irrelevant to the advance of God's kingdom. The fact that there was little evidence of these principles 'working' in inner city locations did not seem to make any difference.

Some would go further than this. There have been so-called prophecies calling the faithful out of the cities because of the wickedness there. They are regarded as ripe for judgement, prime targets for nuclear warfare or whatever other means God may use to punish them.

But these negative views of the inner city need to be challenged. While there are certainly environmental and social problems there are many positive aspects also. The warmth and openness that still exist in many city communities contrast very positively with the cold individualism of the commuter belt. Furthermore, we need to reckon with the evidence from various studies of suburban life that suggest these areas have their own problems. These studies refer to 'too much socialising, useless hyperactivity in voluntary associations, competition and conspicuous consumption. Many of these evils are thought to be the result of boredom.' The reports warn that the suburban way of life is 'so full of stress that it increases psychosomatic illness, divorce, alcoholism, suicide attempts and mental illnesses generally.'[6]

It must also be recognised that in large measure the inner cities are as they are because the suburbs are as they are. Inner city problems are not all created by those who live there. The bad decisions, corruption and indifference of those who work in the city centres and live in the suburbs have contributed to the state of the inner cities. Economic, social and spiritual resources from outside the inner city are needed to compensate for the injustice and neglect that have produced the problems there.

In the same way the weakness of the Church in the urban areas is the responsibility of the whole Church. It is not just the responsibility of inner city Christians, many of whom are trying faithfully and courageously to be part of the solution to the needs of their city. They very much need the support, encouragement and involvement of the wider Church.

I believe that an understanding of the Bible's teaching on the city can help the Church to challenge these negative attitudes and to release personnel and resources for urban mission. There is no concept of 'inner city' in the Bible, but looking at the references to the city can give us an overview of urban life and show us where the inner city fits in. Some aspects of the Bible's strategy for winning the city can be worked out most effectively in the powerful city centres; many others apply naturally and effectively to the zone of powerlessness and deprivation that surrounds those centres.

Different Christians will be called to different ministries in the city – a few may even be called to the suburbs! If the focus in the following chapters is on the inner city, this is not because other areas are unimportant or because I am equating the city with the inner city. It is because it is in the inner city that there is the most desperate need and most glorious opportunity to respond to the biblical teaching. Human logic might suggest that an urban strategy should concentrate on the powerful city centres, but throughout the Bible and church history God has surprised His people by using a 'bottom up' approach and choosing the weak, poor and despised. If this is true also in God's urban mission, then the inner city is the key to the cities.

PART II

The City in the Bible

Chapter 3

The City in the Old Testament

The building of cities is not a modern phenomenon. Hardly have Adam and Eve been expelled from the garden when their son, Cain, begins to build a city. In the period just after the Flood several other cities are mentioned, including the infamous Babel. Nimrod is named as a city-building warrior-king. The roots of urbanisation can be traced back almost to the dawn of human history.

But what does the term 'city' mean in the Bible? Can we make any valid connection between these early settlements and the huge industrial, political and economic centres of our time? The Hebrew word translated 'city' can refer to various kinds of settlements, some of which were probably no more than walled villages. So we need to take care how we apply biblical texts to modern cities. But the essential function of cities has not changed. Even the earliest cities were power centres with a significant influence on the surrounding area. Indeed, as is often the case with prototypes, some features of city life can be seen more clearly in these early cities than in later more complex ones.

Furthermore it is known that some early cities were quite extensive. Nineveh had around 100,000 citizens by the time of Jonah: it was probably made up of three settlements – Calah, Resen and Nineveh itself. This may be the first recorded example of urban sprawl and the erosion of the green belt!

What then does the Bible mean by the term 'city'?

(1) Cities, especially capital cities, are often regarded as representing nations. When the prophets speak to Damascus,

their words are for the whole nation of Syria. We are quite familiar with this. When news reports speak of Washington or Moscow doing things we are hearing about American or Russian activities, rather than something restricted to two cities. Cities are national focal points. The Bible recognises their strategic significance – the Church needs to do the same.

(2) Cities are regarded as 'corporate personalities', not just collections of individuals. Western individualism finds this concept hard to cope with but it is a key element in the biblical narrative. Judgement, responsibility for sin, repentance and blessing take place at city level as well as among individuals. If a prophet calls a city to repent, it is the city as a whole which must respond. Some citizens may be personally guilty, others may be tolerating sin, still others may be its victims – but they are all part of a sinful city. Godly individuals can make a difference, as we shall see, but the corporate personality of the city is an aspect of biblical revelation that is important we come to terms with.

(3) The Bible speaks not only about various cities but about 'the city' as an institution or spiritual reality. Particularly in Hebrews and Revelation the city is a symbol as well as a geographical feature. The city stands for the world without God, secular culture, the exclusion of moral and spiritual absolutes. Each city has unique characteristics and its own distinctive history, but all cities manifest the same 'urban spirit'. This is clear from the final chapters of Revelation: all the cities of the Earth are identified with Babylon the Great. When she falls, they all collapse too. The city is the world in concentrated form.

(4) The Bible is not anti-urban. It is even-handed, seeing value and corruption in both city and countryside. Its vision of the future contains both urban and rural elements, though the centrepiece is the City of God. But the Bible recognises that there is something distinctive about the city, a difference of degree. *'The whole world is under the control of the evil one,'*[1] but his headquarters appear to be in the city. Sin is present everywhere, but it is concentrated and reaches its most virulent form in the city. The cities are spiritual focal points where key spiritual battles are fought.

With this as our frame of reference, we can start where the Bible starts – with Cain, the first city-builder.

Cain, Nimrod and Babel

'Then the Lord said to Cain, "Where is your brother Abel?"
"I don't know," he replied. "Am I my brother's keeper?"
The Lord said, "What have you done? Listen! Your
brother's blood cries out to me from the ground ... which
opened its mouth to receive your brother's blood from your
hand. When you work the ground, it will no longer yield its
crops for you. You will be a restless wanderer on the
earth."'
(Genesis 4:9–12)

It was this final sentence that appalled Cain most. As we read on we find that God in mercy promised to put a mark on Cain to protect him, but Cain had other ideas. He went out from the presence of God and built a city (Genesis 4:16–17). Not content with an invisible mark of security, he built a very visible place of refuge. How do we interpret this? Was it a justifiable attempt to ease the consequences of what he had done? The development of pain killers to help women in childbirth and the invention of agricultural machinery to help people work the ground have been welcomed by most Christians (though both were once frowned upon in churches as attempts to evade the consequences of the Fall).

A close examination of this chapter suggests, however, that building a city was a further act of defiance and disobedience. Refusing to accept his punishment and rejecting God's offer of security, Cain builds his city, a symbol of self-sufficiency and independence. Built well away from the presence of the Lord, the city is named after Cain's son as an expression that Cain's family and future are bound up in the city he has built. At a time when the Bible tells us that *'men began to call upon the name of the Lord'* (Genesis 4:26), the building of this city was an attempt by Cain to 'perpetuate his own name in the self-sustaining security of his city.'[2]

This is not a promising start. The city represents men and women's alternative to fellowship with God, their attempt to feel secure and significant. Conceived in sin and defiance, it is birthed away from God's presence as if to exclude him. It is a concrete expression of self-reliance but a symbol also of alienation. Alienated from the ground, men and women create a new environment for themselves; alienated from other human beings, they build walls to surround themselves; alienated from God they create a new little world to have dominion over. The city is their kingdom, their pride and joy, their greatest achievement – and yet, as we shall see, the place where they are the least secure and most alienated.

The second city-builder was Nimrod, who built several cities including Nineveh (Genesis 10:8–12). Although details of his life are few, it seems clear that he was an aggressive warrior-king who built cities to strengthen and perhaps adorn the lands he conquered. Cain built a city to settle in and for protection against his enemies, but Nimrod's cities seem to have been centres of military power from which to launch assaults or to dominate subject territories. If Cain's city speaks of security, Nimrod's cities represent domination: both symbolise human achievement and self-assertion. North American cities with 'Fort' in their names recall a similar military origin.

The most famous and significant of the early cities is Babel. We are given considerable information about the motivation behind its construction, and for the first time we discover something of the Lord's response to city building. *'Come, let's build ourselves a city, with a tower that reaches to the heavens, so that we may make a name for ourselves and not be scattered over the face of the whole earth,'* say the builders (Genesis 11:4). Do you notice the similarity to Cain's motives – to make a name, and to avoid being wanderers? The famous tower was a way of saying, 'Who needs a god if we can build our way to heaven?'

The builders' enthusiasm is evident, but their work is in vain. The God they have written off intervenes and the very thing they feared comes to pass. Their language is confused, their unity and security are shattered and they are dispersed. Why does the Lord intervene? It is usually assumed that the pride of the builders was offensive to Him, but perhaps this should be seen as a merciful intervention, slowing down the speed of human achievement to limit their potential to harm themselves and their world.

The unfinished building work at Babel is symbolic of the fact that no city in history has ever been finished. The city is always a goal rather than an achievement. Spoilt by sin, the city can never fully replace the lost presence of God or satisfy the aspirations of human beings. The city fails to provide a genuine answer to the problems of wandering and insecurity. Only the city of God, which is perfect from its foundation, can provide this. But that lies much further down the road.

Judgement on the City

The rest of the Old Testament introduces us to many other cities, some of which we will look at in detail later, and reveals more of the Lord's response to their building. We will not be surprised after what we have seen already to find that the city is often under judgement, but there are a number of more positive comments also. Cities are products of human creativity, skill and industry. Like the human race the cities are warped and corrupted but they retain vitality and potential for good. Several passages celebrate the beauty, architecture and culture of cities.[3] The order and security they provide are valuable. Even when judgement is pronounced over the city, it is with sadness not pleasure. The biblical writers are not anti-urban, contrasting the horrors of the city with the merits of rural areas. The aversion many Christians have to the city is not justified by biblical evidence.

There is potential in the city for both good and evil. Whatever the motives behind the building of cities and whatever they symbolise, human beings made in God's image cannot help producing things of value, even in their rebellion and independence. Cities are worth saving. They may be built to the glory of men and women rather than the glory of God, but there is a glory about them which is worth redeeming. God's heart for the cities of the human race is not to destroy them but to redeem them. This is of fundamental significance for urban mission.

But the Old Testament is realistic about the sins of the city. The prophets highlight many different sins and each city has its own particular weakness – the militarism of Nineveh, the sexual perversion of Sodom, the gross affluence of Tyre. But from hundreds of references five main sins stand out.

(1) Oppression

The unjust treatment of the poor by the rich, the weak by the strong, the citizens by their rulers. Using violence, bribery, slander and extortion, oppressors dominate the cities. Many prophets warn of judgement on this behaviour.[4] *'Woe to the city of oppressors, rebellious and defiled!'* cries Zephaniah (Zephaniah 3:1).

(2) Idolatry

This was not confined to the city; at times the countryside was full of idols. But the prophets speak out clearly against urban idolatry.[5] Jeremiah imagines people walking past ruined Jerusalem and asking, *'Why has the Lord done such a thing to this great city?'* The answer they will receive is that the city *'worshipped and served other gods'* (Jeremiah 22:8–9).

(3) Bloodshed

Cities are places of violence where the weak suffer and innocent blood is shed. Twice Ezekiel calls out *'Woe to the city of bloodshed'* and declares that:

> *'the blood shed is in her midst: she poured it on the bare rock; she did not pour it on the ground, where the dust would cover it.'*   (Ezekiel 24:6–9)

Are there echoes here of the blood of Abel crying out from the ground against the first city-builder? It is particularly the shedding of innocent blood that makes the city ripe for judgement.[6]

(4) Sexual immorality

Sodom and Gomorrah are infamous for their sexual perversion but many other cities were centres of vice and sexual sin.[7] In one of the most revolting chapters in the Bible Ezekiel compares the immorality of Jerusalem unfavourably with the behaviour of Sodom (Ezekiel 16). It is worth noting that in this chapter, as elsewhere, the sins of injustice and sexual immorality are exposed and condemned together. There is a tendency in the Church to emphasise one at the expense of the other, but sexual purity and social justice are both important to urban life.

(5) Pride

It is the arrogance and stubbornness of the city which hinder it from responding to God. Zephaniah captures the spirit of the city when he writes of Nineveh,

> *'This is the carefree city that lived in safety. She said to herself, "I am, and there is none besides me."'*
> (Zephaniah 2:15)

This is the language of divinity and of overweening pride.[8]

What is our response to this list? To despair of the city? To write it off? It surely cannot be to assume that our cities are any better. Cities are still places where the poor and powerless get a raw deal. They are still centres of sexual 'freedom' and exploitation. Temples to Mammon dominate urban skylines as completely as any idols held sway in ancient cities. The violence and bloodshed in our inner cities have become all too familiar, and the prophecies about the destruction of the innocent are very apt to the abortion of thousands of unborn babies in our cities. And civic pride still counts for much in those places where the equally dangerous spirit of nationalism has not taken over.

We may not sit in judgement nor need we give way to despair. The good news is that though He hates the city's sins God loves the city and has not abandoned it. It is important we discover the balance of the biblical treatment of the city. Go too far in either direction and you will hate the city or justify its sins. The city is under judgement – but judgement is not inevitable. God has a strategy to rescue the city, and it is to this we now turn.

Hope for the City

'The earth is the Lord's, and everything in it,' declares the Psalmist (Psalm 24:1). In spite of the sin of the human race and the activities of Satan, God has not given up one square foot of the world He made and loves. This includes the cities. So many of our songs use rural images that it has been a real encouragement to me to march around inner city housing estates singing the lines of British song writer, Graham Kendrick's song:

'The earth is the Lord's ... the cities and towns, the houses and streets.'

God has not disowned the city. He will act to reclaim it for His kingdom. There are several signs of hope for the city in the Old Testament.

(1) God loves the city

Scattered through the Old Testament are several references to this. His love for Jerusalem is well-known but Damascus also is called *'the town in which I delight'* (Jeremiah 49:25), and Jonah is rebuked for failing to share God's concern for Nineveh. A vital ingredient of urban ministry is a God-given love for the city.

(2) The ministry of the prophets

'Listen,' cries Micah (Micah 6:9), *'The Lord is calling to the city.'* Though often His call was to warn of judgement, the point is that God cared enough for the city to send messengers to it. Several prophets, in fact, received thrilling revelations of urban life as it could be with the Lord at its head. The city of God is the central feature of the Old Testament vision of a restored land, a city without walls but totally secure.[9]

(3) God uses the city

Psalm 107 celebrates the benefits of city life, contrasting it with life in the desert and hostile countryside: it is portrayed as God's solution to human needs. In spite of its rebellious origin, God graciously adopts the city and uses it to rescue the needy. This gives us hope.

> 'The very fact that God has called the city into his service – man's exclusive work and spiritual power in rebellion against God – is a proclamation of coming reconciliation.'[10]

(4) The Cities of Refuge

The setting up of the Cities of Refuge (Joshua 20:1–9) is a very significant example of God's willingness to use the city. He not only deigns to use cities built by men and women, He even uses them in a similar way. Cain had built a city as a refuge. Now God was establishing refuges – but with the significant difference that they were only for inadvertent killers. Cain would not have found refuge there. This is redemptive, to make use of the city in a way which honours the original motive behind its building but without compromise. The city is not transformed out of all recognition: unrighteous features are removed, but all that is positive and useful about it is affirmed.

(5) *The city of Jerusalem*

The centrepiece of God's recovery plan in the Old Testament was Jerusalem. His response to the development of cities was not to retreat to the countryside but to establish His own city. Jerusalem, the city of God, was intended to be a radical alternative, a city set on a hill to show what a city could be like. What Israel was to be at a national level, Jerusalem was to be at an urban level, a model of justice, joy and peace.

Israel had not been a city-building nation. Apart from the enforced construction of cities in Egypt, they had not started building their own cities until the time of Solomon. They had inherited their earlier cities from the Canaanites. God had in a remarkable way protected them from the lure of city-building. It was only when other things started going wrong that Israel copied other nations by developing a city-building programme.

Jerusalem therefore was not of Israelite construction. Indeed it was one of the last cities in Canaan to be captured by Israel. Hardly a worthy history for a capital city! But that was the point. God chose for His city a place that had no history, that could give Israel no reason to take pride in their achievements. The crucial thing about this city was not its history but its destiny.

Several psalms speak of Jerusalem in glowing terms,[11] in marked contrast to the prophets' estimation of other cities. Psalm 87 shows us people clamouring to be admitted as citizens of this joyful city of God. Jerusalem was a concrete sign that God had not rejected the city, a working model of the New Jerusalem that was coming.

Disappointment and Hope

One of the tragedies of the Old Testament is that Jerusalem fails to fulfil its destiny. All the sins associated with other cities are to be found in her too.[12] In some ways she is worse than the others considering the height from which she had fallen. The prophets sounded warnings but Israel refused to give heed, secure in the assumption that God would not allow His city to fall. But fall it did, and the citizens are carried away to ... Babylon. As we shall see, Babylon is the symbol of human rebellion beyond all other cities, standing in direct opposition to all that Jerusalem stood for. But if the people of Jerusalem are going to live *like* the citizens of Babylon, they might as well live *in* Babylon. The irony of the failure of Jerusalem is that God should use a city such as Babylon to be His instrument of judgement.

God's recovery plan seems to have ground to a halt. As the Old Testament draws to a close the city of Jerusalem is a pale shadow of its former glory. The walls have been rebuilt and the temple restored, but there is little vision or prospect of Jerusalem influencing anyone. It was an object of scorn, not a place of renown.

But still the prophets give us hope. Several speak of a restoration following judgement.[13] Jerusalem may have failed but God's purpose will be fulfilled. A new Jerusalem will come which will demonstrate God's purpose for urban life. The recovery plan will take off again with the angels' announcement:

> '*To you is born this day in the city of David a Saviour who is Christ the Lord.*' (Luke 2:11)

With the coming of Jesus God's rescue plan for the human race and its cities enters a new phase. But before we turn to this, we must address another issue – who rules in the city?

35

Chapter 4

Who Rules the City?

Urban graffiti is usually regarded as one of the unpleasant features of inner cities. It is certainly a nuisance for those required to remove it and much of it is filthy, racist or banal. But occasionally a graffiti artist puts his or her finger on something that deserves to be expressed and pondered, and for many people daubing it on a wall is the only way to do this. I have a great deal of sympathy with the anonymous Londoner who renamed the Department of Health and Social Security as 'The Department of Stealth and Total Obscurity'. On several occasions as I have tried to help people with housing or social security problems, I have been shunted back and forth between different departments until I have returned to square one. There seems to be nobody willing to say, 'I am in charge here.'

The question we will be exploring in this chapter is: 'Who actually runs the city?' The city is clearly a power structure, but where is the power located? Since there are pointers towards an answer in both Testaments we will look at this issue here before moving on to look at how Jesus dealt with the cities.

The city, as we have seen, was built by human beings as their kingdom, where they could work out their own plans without divine interference. So we would expect to find men and women in charge of the city, ruling over it and using its resources for their own projects. But various biblical passages and careful observation of our cities suggest that there is more to it than this.

One obvious qualification is that power within the city is always concentrated in the hands of a very few. Those with the political, economic, academic or military muscle are able to dominate the city and harness its resources. Those without such power may experience the city in a different way, as an oppressive and inhuman place. The truth is that the city is a divided kingdom, divided between the 'haves' and the 'have nots', those able to manipulate the urban power structures and those who suffer from such manipulation.

The prophets spoke out against the injustice of this, and Jesus warned that any kingdom which is divided against itself is in danger of collapse. The city is not as stable as it often appears, nor does it fulfil its potential for large numbers of its inhabitants. For the urban poor the city is not a refuge but a place of oppression, a place of vulnerability rather than strength and security. The city that humanity made has turned against it and is slowly throttling it.

But in any human society some wield power over others. What is it about the city that makes this relationship so distorted and damaging? Perhaps the central problem is the lack of accountability and personal involvement. The city seems to be ruled by 'faceless bureaucrats', anonymous departments and complex systems that deal with numbers rather than people. Large modern cities exhibit this much more than in earlier times, and it is those in the inner city who are worst affected.

Decisions are made by those who live far away and will not suffer the consequences. Those who do suffer become bitter, frustrated and eventually apathetic when it seems impossible to find the 'right' person to contact. The result of such a system is frequently incompetence, laziness and corruption.

The graffiti artist was expressing a deeply felt complaint. I am sure there are individual exceptions, but by and large the exercise of power in the city is not in trustworthy hands. From time to time attempts are made to effect radical changes, to root out corruption, to humanise systems; but these turn out to be superficial, shifting the furniture around but sometimes making matters even worse. Even those in charge seem powerless to make real changes. The system is so strong and resilient that even the powerful seem helpless.

It is at this point that we need to look at the way in which the Bible speaks about power in the city. The city is not just a shorthand for those who live in it. It is more than the sum total of the citizens, their homes and possessions. The city has a corporate personality, a life of its own, that transcends its component parts. God speaks both to the city and to its citizens – and He may not say the same things to both.

In Revelation we are introduced to Babylon the Great in a revolting vision of a prostitute drunk with human blood. Many cities in the Bible are given a female corporate personality, but the fascinating phrase used about this urban personality is that she is

> *'the great city that **rules over** the kings of the earth.'*
> (Revelation 17:18)

We would normally think of kings ruling over their cities, and this is certainly what kings imagine they are doing. But the Bible tells us that the truth is the opposite: it is the city which rules over them!

The city, the creation of the human race, has grown powerful and is now out of control. Just as in the science fiction story where robots made by human beings usurp their authority and take over the world, so in reality the city has taken over.

This helps us to understand what is happening in our cities. No wonder urban problems seem so immense, so insoluble. No wonder changes of government and personnel make so little real difference. The systems and institutions of the city have a life of their own, which people service but cannot control. Indeed the paradox is that the more powerful the individual, the more fully he or she is serving the city. Human beings are in slavery in their own cities – and most people have no idea that this is so.

But where does this power come from that runs the city? So far we have looked at the city in the Bible purely at a human level. It is time we looked behind the scenes at the spiritual or supernatural dimension of the city.

The Power Behind the City

There are two important Old Testament prophecies which give us some insight into this dimension: the prophecy against the

king of Babylon in Isaiah 14, and the prophecy to the ruler of
Tyre in Ezekiel 28. In both there is interaction of natural and
supernatural elements: it is rather like looking at a photograph
with double exposure. Sometimes the distinction is clear but in
many places it is blurred.

The prophecy in Isaiah 14 is described as a 'taunt' (v. 3). The
setting is Sheol, the realm of the dead. The prophet imagines
the ruler of Babylon arriving there to be met by a welcoming
committee of world leaders, many of whom had been conquered by Babylon. *'You also have become weak, as we are; you
have become like us,'* they greet him. The prophecy assures
those who have been oppressed that Babylon will fall and its
ruler will die like all mortals. This is the essence of the prophecy
on the human level, but in the middle of it we find several
phrases which seem to take us into a different dimension.

> *'How have you fallen from heaven, O morning star, son of
> the dawn! You have been cast down to the earth ... You said
> in your heart, "I will ascend to heaven; I will raise my
> throne above the stars of God; I will sit enthroned on the
> mount of assembly, on the utmost heights of the sacred
> mountain ... I will make myself like the Most High."'*
>
> (Isaiah 14:12–14)

What are we to make of this? It is certainly true that the
Babylonian rulers considered themselves semi-divine and were
fond of speaking in grandiose language about themselves, but
there does seem to be more to this passage than human
arrogance. Many commentators have seen here glimpses of a
shadowy figure standing behind the earthly ruler. Some have
identified him as Satan himself, aspiring to be like the Almighty
and being thrown out of heaven. The earthly ruler is cast down
to Sheol, the spiritual figure is cast down to earth: they are
related but distinct. Whoever the spiritual figure is – Satan
himself or a 'power' behind the city – the point is that this city
has a supernatural dimension as well as a natural one. These
dimensions reinforce each other: the destiny of the city is bound
up with what takes place in the spiritual realm as well as with
events on earth.

The same mixture of natural and supernatural is to be found in the 'lament' over the king of Tyre in Ezekiel 28. In the early verses we find several references to the self-glorying and blasphemous claims of the earthly ruler (vv. 2, 6, 9) and a very firm rebuttal:

> *'You will be but a man not a god in the hands of those who slay you.'*
> (Ezekiel 28:9)

The prophet sees that the cities and their rulers are temporary and finite.

But in the later verses the focus has shifted to another figure:

> *'You were the model of perfection, full of wisdom and perfect in beauty. You were in Eden, the garden of God ... You were anointed as a guardian cherub ... You were on the holy mount of God ... Your heart became proud on account of your beauty, and you corrupted your wisdom because of your splendour. So I threw you to the earth.*
> (Ezekiel 28:12–17)

This must surely be a spiritual being, probably Satan himself, whose influence is behind the earthly ruler of Tyre.

Urban Hijacking

Why do people not feel fully at home in their cities? Why are their attitudes to them so ambivalent? Men and women flock to the cities in search of homes, work, glamour, entertainment and enlightenment, but many find loneliness, misery, exploitation and poverty. As some move in, many others move out to the suburbs and beyond, eager to escape urban pressures. Why does the city seem not only inadequate but hostile and oppressive? Human sin plays a part in this but there is another factor.

The truth is that Satan has hijacked the city. Just as he invaded the garden to spoil God's beautiful creation, so he has pounced on the city and wrested control from men and women, ruining the city in the process. The corruption of the city was the easier task: it was already facing away from God, trying to shut Him out. Made for human beings, it is purpose built for Satan who gratefully moves in and takes over. The city will be his instrument now, a powerful tool in his campaign to erase the image of God from the earth and to keep men and women from God's presence.

We know from the Bible that Satan has been thrown out of heaven and consigned to the earth. A wanderer like Cain he is described as

'roaming through the earth and going to and fro in it.'[1]

Just as the human race lost Eden so Satan lost heaven. Humanity has built itself a new home but Satan and his forces have moved in.

We are not to think that Satan operates only in cities, any more than seeing human sin as confined to cities. But just as the cities are places where human sin is concentrated, so too they are centres of operation for demonic powers. The cities are not only military power bases – they are centres of spiritual warfare also. When Jesus speaks to the church at Pergamum He says,

'I know where you live – where Satan has his throne.'

A little later He refers to a martyr

'who was put to death in your city – where Satan lives.'
(Revelation 2:12–13)

In what way is Satan involved in the city? He is certainly involved at a personal level, attacking the people of God and obstructing their ministry there. He is quick to seize any opportunity to gain influence in the lives of individuals and in their homes. Demonic oppression is by no means confined to the cities but it is prevalent there. Many urban areas have a history of occult practices going back for generations. The number of 'haunted houses' that we have been asked to deal with is an indication to us of the legacy of such activities. The modern resurgence of interest in such things is preparing the way for the description of the city found in Revelation:

41

'she has become a home for demons and a haunt for every evil spirit.'[2]

Could it be that the prevalence of occult activity in the city and the weakness of the Church in the city are connected? There are some inner city areas which have never had a significant Christian population. The occupying demonic forces have never been effectively challenged. And what of the exploding megacities in Africa, Asia and Latin America, where too often the focus of mission is still on rural areas? While the Church at large ignores this situation the forces of darkness continue to make their 'home' in the city. It is time we woke up to the outrage and disgrace that this situation represents.

But Satan's involvement in the city is not just at a personal level. David wrote that *'destructive forces are at work in the city.'*[3] These forces are at work in the structures and systems of the city. It is these that give the city its independent character and oppressive atmosphere. The subject of 'principalities and powers' has provoked renewed interest in recent years with much debate as to whether these are supernatural beings or references to structural forces. My own belief is that they are both; there are supernatural intelligences involved, which work through the institutions and power structures of human society. The city is a primary human structure and as such is one of the main spheres of operation of 'the powers'. The increasingly popular phrase 'territorial spirits' does point to this dimension of evil beyond the individual level, but a more sophisticated analysis than territoriality is needed of the ways in which evil is manifested in a complex entity like a modern city.

So we return to the question: who rules the city? We have suggested that the answer is quite complex, for there is both human and spiritual power involved. Human beings believe they rule over the cities but the Bible tells us the cities rule over them. This is made possible by the intervention of spiritual powers which were intended to act constructively but have become corrupt and oppressive. Satan makes use of these powers and of the structures of human cities in his implacable campaign against the God he tried but failed to usurp. Men and women cannot escape responsibility for their cities and their sins, but it is important to understand that there is a spiritual dimension involved which exacerbates the city's problems. David Sheppard, now Bishop of Liverpool, wrote several years ago:

> 'I have not discovered a better way of describing the power of evil after eighteen years' ministry in London than the Bible's name of Satan ... demonic intelligence seems to be behind so much evil which confronts us.'[4]

The Church needs to reckon with this dimension if it is to be effective in urban ministry. Alone among agencies at work in the city it has the ability to discern these spiritual forces and to wage war against them. One of the reasons for the present weakness in urban ministry is the failure to take this dimension seriously and to develop an appropriate response. We will return to this theme in a later chapter.

Who Really Rules?

But the final answer to the question of who rules the city is different from all we have said so far. If we stop here we have nothing but an uphill struggle ahead. We see the city full of idols, dominated by unseen and destructive forces, with even the most powerful individuals unwittingly doing the bidding of these malignant forces. To be quite honest, urban ministry does at times feel like this.

But the final answer is that actually Jesus rules the city. He told His disciples,

> *'all authority in heaven and on earth has been given to me.'*[5]

He has disarmed the powers, exposed their activities and their weaknesses, and triumphed over them on the cross. The power of the city was defeated on the cross, along with all other powers. Their activities continue and even increase as the age draws to a close, but they have been defeated. The size and number of the cities may increase, the problems within them may be multiplied, the effects of urbanisation may seem all-embracing, but the powers cannot win. Jesus rules over the city.

We may see little of the rule of Jesus in our cities at present, but our task as His disciples is to declare and to demonstrate in the heart of the city that Jesus is Lord. If the Church fails to do this and continues to retreat to the suburbs, the vacuum that is left will soon be filled by other forces which are already laying claim to the cities.

It is crucial we understand what the Bible teaches us about the powers at work in the city, but crucial too that we are not daunted by this. Paul speaks of the powers as being 'weak and miserable'.[6] The challenge of the cities may seem huge to us. We may react like the spies who reported about the land of Canaan:

> *'the people who live there are powerful, and the cities are fortified and very large.'*

Where are those with the spirit of Caleb, who silenced this fearful talk and declared,

> *'We should go up and take possession of the land, for we can certainly do it.'*   (Numbers 13:28–30)

Jesus rules over the city and He is calling His people to believe that and to go into the city and meet Him there, to demonstrate His rule and to reveal His presence to those who have not yet found Him. We must follow Him wherever He leads, among the powerless and the seemingly powerful, to the urban priority areas and the commercial city centres. But before we do this we must see how He brought the good news of the kingdom to the cities of His day.

Chapter 5

Jesus and the City

Jesus the Wanderer

Jesus was born in a city, but in a city which had no political, economic or military significance. Bethlehem was famous as the family home of David but nothing much had happened there since. All the action took place in nearby Jerusalem. The small size of Bethlehem is the one feature noted in Micah's prophecy of where the Messiah would be born (Micah 5:2). Jesus came into our urban situation but chose to do so in a place that only just qualified as a city.

And even in Bethlehem there was no room for Him. Throughout history the city had made no room for God, eager to exclude Him from this place of human self-sufficiency. The only place available in Bethlehem was a stable, possibly the most rural feature of the city. The baby's first visitors were the shepherds, men not really at home in the city. But God had never accepted His exclusion from the city and in Jesus He was breaking in again in a more dynamic way than ever before.

Herod's reaction to the news typifies the city's response:

'he was disturbed, and all Jerusalem with him.'

(Matthew 2:3).

The city is unsettled. Herod is threatened and attempts to regain control, first by manipulating the wise men then by lashing out with indiscriminate violence. He fails to destroy Jesus but he forces Him to flee from the city, and as is so often the case it was the vulnerable and powerless who suffered the consequences of the city's rejection of God (Matthew 2:16).

From then on Jesus' life was characterised by movement. The only period when He was settled – growing up in Nazareth – is passed over in total silence. His earliest years were marked by wandering and uncertainty; from Nazareth to Bethlehem in His mother's womb; to Egypt to escape Herod; then back to the comparative safety of Nazareth. Our only glimpse of His childhood shows Jesus travelling again and going astray on the way home (Luke 2:41–52).

After His baptism the Spirit leads Jesus into the desert, the start of three years of wandering around the towns and villages of Galilee, Samaria and Judea, ministering in various cities but settling in none. He tells a would-be follower:

> *'the Son of Man has nowhere to lay his head.'* (Luke 9:58)

On occasions people try to persuade Him to settle but He refuses to be deterred from His mission:

> *'... and would have kept him from leaving them; but he said to them, "I must preach the good news of the kingdom of God to the other cities also; for I was sent for this purpose."'*
> (Luke 4:42–43)

He has a mission to the cities but He will not settle in them.

What is the significance of this wandering? Was it simply a way of avoiding hostility and danger? Jesus refused to be excluded from the cities but He did not deliberately court danger (John 7:1). He knew the city's rulers were threatened by Him and He was well aware of the power of the mob – an essentially urban phenomenon. There would be a time to confront the power of the city, but not yet.

Or could there be a deeper significance? Could it be that Jesus was not only the 'last Adam' (1 Corinthians 15:45) but the last Cain also? Cain was placed under a curse and told he would be a wanderer, but he refused to accept this and built a city instead. Jesus, who came to undo every curse on humankind took Cain's place and accepted a life of wandering, trusting as

Cain failed to do in the promise of His Father's protection and provision. In doing this He declares His freedom from the power of the city and breaks the hold of the city and its false security that has beguiled the human race.

No wonder then that Satan tried to get Jesus to compromise with the city. He took Jesus to the city and urged Him to leap off the temple, performing a miracle by landing unharmed (Luke 4:9–11). Such a feat would 'make a name' for Jesus and launch a successful ministry. This temptation to seek a reputation in the city recurs later: His sceptical brothers tell Him,

> *'You ought to leave here and go to Judea, so that your disciples may see the miracles you do. No one who wants to become a public figure acts in secret. Since you are doing these things, show yourself to the world.'*   (John 7:3-4)

The implication here is that it is only in the city that progress can be made: the city is 'the world', the place that really matters. Reputation in the city is the key to success. One of the original motives behind the building of cities was just this – 'let us make a name for ourselves'. Jesus rejects this temptation and chooses the way of the powerless wanderer. He will not be identified with the city: if He is to fulfil His mission to the city He must remain independent of it. Just as Christians are called to be 'in the world but not of it', so Jesus is often found 'in the city' but He is not a man 'of the city'.

Woe to the City

Jesus' ministry had a significant urban dimension to it. We are accustomed to think of His miracles in rural settings, but it was in the cities (of Korazin, Bethesda and Capernaum) that most of His miracles were performed (Matthew 11:20). These were signs of God's kingdom coming near to the cities and demonstrations of His love for their citizens. Jesus embodied God's persistent mission to the city.

But the cities refused to repent and welcome Jesus. Matthew and Luke both record His solemn words to them as He stands in the prophetic tradition. He compares them with the cities of Tyre, Sidon and Sodom, all of whom would have repented if they had seen these miracles. He pronounces a 'woe' against them and warns them that on the day of judgement they will receive a more severe punishment than those cities because they had rejected Him (Matthew 11:20–24; Luke 10:12–15).

Jesus is the supreme revelation of the Father's character and will, so as we trace the theme of the city through the Bible we would expect to find what is suggested in the Old Testament confirmed, clarified and transcended in Jesus' ministry. How do His words here do this?

First, Jesus addresses cities rather than individuals. He treats them as corporate entities responsible for their lack of repentance. It is not that no individuals in the cities responded to Him but that the cities as a whole rejected Him.

Second, Jesus speaks the word 'woe' to the cities, a solemn denunciation not used lightly in the Bible but normally aimed at those who rely on a security other than God. Jesus agrees with the prophets that the city is under judgement.

Third, He adds to the list of the sins of the city another sin – the failure to recognise God's Son. The miracles were signs that pointed to Him but they had been ignored. Elsewhere Jesus compares His own generation with the city of Nineveh: that city repented at Jonah's preaching but contemporary cities had rebuffed one who was greater than Jonah and thus invited condemnation.

Fourth, the comparison between ancient and contemporary cities is a warning to us that we dare not relegate what the Bible says about the nature of the city to ancient history. Our cities are characterised by the same sins and worse. Whatever improvements modern cities might claim, the biblical trend is a decline into greater wickedness and degeneracy – except where the kingdom of God breaks in.

Finally, there is a word of hope in what is otherwise a solemn passage. Jesus says,

> *'if the miracles that were performed in you had been performed in Sodom, it would have remained to this day.'*
> (Matthew 11:23)

Sodom could have been saved! There was a way, unavailable at that time, for a ministry of miracles would have led to repentance. There is hope for wicked cities when the power of God is manifested. We will return to this later.

Jesus and Jerusalem

Jesus acknowledges the special place Jerusalem once had in the plans of God. He tells His disciples not to swear by it, because it is the *'city of the Great King'* (Matthew 5:35). As He approaches the city He cries out,

> *'If you, even you, had only known on this day what would bring you peace . . . you did not recognise the time of God's coming to you.'*   (Luke 19:42–44)

Though He predicts its destruction, Jesus' love for the city is very evident. He weeps over it as He speaks of its citizens being slaughtered and its buildings demolished (Luke 19:41). He laments over it:

> *'O Jerusalem, Jerusalem . . . how often I have longed to gather your children together, as a hen gathers her chicks under her wings, but you were not willing.'*
>
>   (Matthew 23:37)

Jesus is no less severe in His judgement than the Old Testament prophets, but there is a new revelation of God's love for the city here.

> 'The tears he shed over the city would be forever sufficient justification for Christian urban ministry.'[1]

But Jerusalem has rejected God's love. Throughout its history it has killed prophets – now it will be the place of Jesus' execution. Jesus wanders no longer but *'resolutely set out for Jerusalem'* (Luke 9:51), saying *'surely no prophet can die outside Jerusalem'* (Luke 13:33). The tragedy of Jerusalem continues: her final act as the special city of God is to reject and crucify His Son. In doing this she shows herself to be like every other city.

The scene is set for a triumphal procession into the heart of the city where many hoped Jesus would be swept to power on a wave of popular support after years of wandering and obscurity. But Jesus has faced and conquered the temptation: He will not ally Himself with the power of the city for to do this would be to fail in His mission. His journey to Jerusalem is in marked contrast to the pride and pomp of the city. He rides on a borrowed donkey, stopping only to weep over the city. When He arrives He speaks about injustice and robbery and drives the money-changers from the temple. The characters at the centre of the stage are children shouting His praises and the blind and lame whom He heals – none of which counted in the city. This is all He does in Jerusalem. He ignores the rich and powerful, neither threatening nor trying to appease them. He will not even stay the night in the city but goes out to Bethany. God's mission to the city does not take the form we would expect: the little people have a key place in it.

A few days later the whole city is in uproar again. The crowd which had shouted *'Hosanna'* before was now a frenzied city mob yelling *'Crucify'*. Jesus is condemned and then taken outside the city walls to be crucified. The city has rejected God once more.

But it was the death of Jesus outside the city that was the unexpected climax of God's rescue plan for the city. His refusal to compromise with the power of the city, His death and resurrection broke its power and released men and women from its grip. Paul writes about Jesus that

> *'having disarmed the powers and authorities, he made a public spectacle of them, triumphing over them by the cross.'* (Colossians 2:15)

The city is one of the powers that has been defeated and exposed through the death and resurrection of Jesus. We can now see it for what it is and need fear it no longer. The city is now caught up in God's great purpose of reconciling all things in heaven and earth to Himself (Colossians 1:20). This will not happen at once but the vision of the New Jerusalem assures us that it will happen. The city will be redeemed, on the basis of the cross, to be a blessing to the human race, a place of justice and joyful security.

An Urban Vision

It is in the light of this new understanding of the city that we can respond to Jesus' own urban vision. Like the prophets He uses several urban pictures as He points the disciples towards the coming kingdom.

In the parable of the Ten Minas (Luke 19:11–27), the reward for faithful servants is to take charge of a number of cities. Having responsibility for several cities in this age might be regarded as at best a chore and at worst a curse, but in the coming age, when they are restored and transformed, having charge of a city will be a wonderful blessing.

Speaking to the church in Philadelphia, Jesus again promises an urban reward. His promise to those who overcome is:

> *'I will write on him the name of my God and the name of the city of my God, the new Jerusalem.'*　　(Revelation 3:12)

The name of this city we know from Ezekiel's prophecy is 'The Lord is There'. The reward for faithfulness is to belong to the city of God, where the presence of God is the central reality.

This may be future but in the meantime, Jesus tells His disciples, they are to be a city set on a hill,[2] a light to the nations. As in some Old Testament prophecies, this will be an unusual city, a city without walls, but it will be the model for the world and its cities to learn from. The Church is to replace Jerusalem as the special city of God. Jesus made it quite clear that Jerusalem had lost this role.[3] From now on it was secular, no longer the Holy City as it had been. The Church is now the city of God, whose mission is to witness to all the cities and nations of the world.

God's mission to the city is entering an exciting new phase, one in which though judgement is still an important factor grace and salvation are to predominate. Jesus spells out to His disciples how they are to fulfil this mission. He sends them into various cities to represent Him and to prepare the way for Him. In Luke 10 detailed instructions are given. They are to go in a spirit that is the very opposite to the spirit of the city. The city represents power, wealth and security, but the disciples are sent out like *'lambs among wolves'*, weak and vulnerable. They are not to take money or provisions with them. They are to work both at a personal and family level (vv. 5–7) and at city level (vv. 8–12). They are to proclaim the good news of the kingdom of God, to bring peace and to perform miracles. If they are rejected by the city (again treated as an entity), they are to warn of coming judgement.

This mission to the cities will continue until Jesus returns. Just as the building of the city is never completed, so it will be with the Church's mission. Jesus tells the disciples:

> *'When you are persecuted in one place, flee to another. I tell you the truth, you will not finish going through the cities of Israel before the Son of Man comes.'*   (Matthew 10:23)

How the Early Church responded to this commission and targeted the cities of the Roman Empire is the subject of the next chapter. But it is important that we recognise that Jesus is the turning point in the battle for the city. His death seemed to be the final triumph of the city, its most significant success in excluding God. But the reverse was true. The death and resurrection of Jesus defeated the powers of darkness, among them the power over the city, and brought into being a new kind of city, with Jesus Himself as its foundation stone. God's recovery plan is back on track.

Chapter 6

The Church and the City

The Day of Pentecost

'Stay in the city,' Jesus told the disciples, *'until you have been clothed with power from on high'* (Luke 24:49). Some days later in a room in Jerusalem the Holy Spirit came upon them and filled them with this power to be His witnesses. I am glad that this wonderful event took place in the heart of the city. It could easily have been otherwise: the disciples might have wished to stay on the mountain where Jesus ascended, or return to Galilee and familiar surroundings. But Jesus sends them back to the city.

The city, the place of human power and self-sufficiency, is chosen as the setting for the Spirit's coming. Christians everywhere need His empowering, but the city is where human independence is most clearly expressed and it is here that the Spirit's invasion begins. We do not need to go out of the city to meet God, for He comes to us where we are. Spiritual awakening, even revival, can happen in the city. The Spirit will not be excluded from the city any more than Jesus or the Father.

One result of the Spirit's coming was that the disciples began to speak in other tongues. Attracted by the noise the Spirit was making, a crowd gathered, a multi-national group in Jerusalem to celebrate Pentecost, who were amazed to hear their own native languages being spoken by these Galileans. *'What does this mean?'* they asked.[1]

It meant, among other things, a reversal of Babel. There God said,

53

> *'let us go down and confuse their language so that they will not understand each other.'* (Genesis 11:7)

Here the Holy Spirit comes down and removes the language barrier so that all could understand the disciples praising God. At Babel the Lord scattered people and they stopped building their city. Now in Jerusalem the crowd gathered and the new city of God, the Church, was built up as thousands became disciples on that day. The events of Pentecost are a sign, a foretaste of the coming city of God where men and women from all nations and language-groups will live in fellowship together in God's presence. Babel warns us that the city of men and women will never be finished; Pentecost assures us that the city of God is being built and will be completed.

But the disciples were not to stay in Jerusalem much longer. They were to set their sights on *'the ends of the earth'* (Acts 1:8). Jerusalem in the Old Testament had been the goal, the climax; the prophets had seen it as the gathering place for the nations. Zechariah writes:

> *'the inhabitants of one city will go to another and say, "Let us go at once to entreat the Lord and seek the Lord Almighty. I myself am going." And many peoples and powerful nations will come to Jerusalem to seek the Lord Almighty and to entreat him.'*[2] (Zechariah 8:21–22)

But Jerusalem had become like all other cities. There was no point in the nations gathering there now – though we may see the gathering at Pentecost as a partial fulfilment of the prophecies.

Jerusalem is no longer the goal but the launching pad, from which the Church will move out. The direction of the mission was away from Jerusalem and before long a thoroughly pagan city, Antioch, was the effective centre of this missionary movement. The Church would look back to Jerusalem with affection but its special place in salvation history was at an end and within a few years it was in ruins. The Church was now the model city – but a city with a difference. Its ministry was mobile: instead of waiting for the nations to come to them, the disciples were to go to the nations. The cities of men and women are fixed and immobile but the city of God is on the move. Eventually the New Jerusalem will descend from heaven, but until then the Church also is to be a city on the move.

Mission to the Cities

The recovery plan for the city is under way again: the book of Acts is largely a record of urban mission and church-planting. The Early Church targeted the cities of the Roman Empire and commissioned its key personnel to work there. It was in the cities that people were found in large numbers, where the gospel could be proclaimed to ready audiences. The cities were centres of information networks, the trend-setters, the strategic places where the Church needed to gain a foothold if its mission was to succeed. They were focal points of opposition too, but nothing would deter the missionaries from them. Nor did they concentrate on the rich and powerful as much urban mission since has: all the evidence suggests that the Early Church was predominantly poor and powerless and that the poor were given a high priority in the mission of the Church.

Following the death of Stephen, who like Jesus was taken out of the city to be executed (Acts 7:58), the Church was scattered. We read of Philip who *'went down to a city in Samaria and proclaimed Christ there'* (Acts 8:5), and then of Saul meeting Jesus on the road to Damascus and being told to *'get up and go into the city, and you will be told what you must do'* (Acts 9:6). This going into the city became the start of a great urban ministry for Paul, but one fraught with difficulties.

The battle for the cities was fierce. On several occasions we read that the *'whole city was in an uproar'* (Acts 19:29),[3] stirred by the preaching of the missionaries. Paul had had to escape from Damascus and before long he too was dragged out of a city to be stoned: unlike Stephen he recovered and *'went back into the city'* (Acts 14:20). There was often a mixed reaction: at Iconium we read that *'the people of the city were divided'* (Acts 14:4). The mission teams caused quite a disturbance in the cities and were in danger from the religious leaders, the secular authorities and the city mob. Paul speaks later of being *'in danger in the city'* (2 Corinthians 11:26) as a regular feature of his ministry.

But no opposition would persuade Paul to change his strategy: the cities must be reached with the gospel. And converts were being made and churches planted – which in due time would reach out from the cities to the surrounding areas. So effective was this urban strategy that the word for a country-dweller – *paganos* – has come to mean pagan, one unreached by the gospel. Today it is our inner cities which seem pagan and unreached but in the Early Church the cities were the centres of Christian activity.

Paul received two direct words from the Lord about his urban ministry, which remain relevant for urban mission today. He says on his way to Jerusalem:

> *'I only know that in every city the Holy Spirit warns me that prison and hardships are facing me.'*   (Acts 20:23)

He was aware of the cost of urban ministry. But he had earlier received a word of encouragement:

> *'Do not be afraid; keep on speaking, do not be silent, for I am with you, and no-one is going to attack and harm you, because I have many people in this city.'*   (Acts 18:9–10)

God has many people in our cities too. Some are struggling to maintain a witness for Him; some are feeling lost and isolated and need to be gathered in to living city churches; some are not yet believers but are waiting to receive the gospel if only the Church would wake up to the opportunities and needs in the city.

An Urban Vision

The Early Church also took up and developed the urban vision of the Old Testament. Beyond their efforts to evangelise their cities they saw with eyes of faith the coming city of God: this was a central theme in their hope and undergirded their mission. Could it be our failure to grasp this that has led to the neglect of many areas of our cities and the evacuation of the Church to the suburbs?

Paul describes the Church as a city as well as a household and a nation. He tells the Philippians *'our citizenship is in heaven'* (Philippians 3:20) – they are not to be finally identified with an earthly city but to be looking towards the city of God in which they have a place as citizens. This detachment is important in urban mission: we must be able to evaluate our city in the light of God's future if we are to serve it faithfully and prophetically. But in no way does this lessen our commitment to the city. It is because of our vision of an urban future that we know the city is worth saving. God has not written the city off nor will we. We do not expect to make the city of God out of the cities of men and women – we have no utopian ideas about the city. But if God's plan for our future centres on a city we can live and work and pray for change in our cities in the light of this.

The author of Hebrews takes up this theme. In the famous chapter about the people of faith in the Old Testament the city emerges as a primary motivation. Abraham left the city of Ur and became a wanderer, living in tents and not knowing where he was going. What was his faith reaching out for?

> *'he was looking forward to the city with foundations, whose architect and builder is God.'*   (Hebrews 11:10)

His descendants also lived in hope of a heavenly homeland and God's response to their faith is that He

> *'is not ashamed to be called their God, for he has prepared a city for them.'*   (Hebrews 11:16)

Heaven is not a rural paradise: at its heart is a wonderful city. In His incredible grace the Creator has become a Builder, taking up the human race's rebellious city project and turning it into the centre-piece of His kingdom.

In the next chapter we read,

> *'you have come to Mount Zion, to the heavenly Jerusalem, the city of the living God. You have come to thousands upon*

thousands of angels in joyful assembly, to the church of the firstborn, whose names are written in heaven.'

(Hebrews 12:22–23)

Our destination is a city thronging with joyful angels and redeemed humanity. The next verse speaks of *'Jesus the mediator of a new covenant'*, through whom we have access to this city. His blood *'speaks a better word than the blood of Abel'*. It was the death of Abel that led to the building of the first city, in which Cain hoped to escape God's presence. Abel's blood cried out for vengeance. But the death of Jesus has led to the founding of this new city, and His blood cries out for forgiveness and salvation so that redeemed men and women can enjoy the presence of God in the new city.

The final chapter contains a further reference:

'Jesus also suffered outside the city gate to make the people holy through his own blood. Let us, then, go to him outside the camp, bearing the disgrace he bore. For here we do not have an enduring city, but we are looking for the city that is to come.'
(Hebrews 13:12–14)

We noticed earlier the death of Jesus outside the city: what was implicit then is explicit now. Just as Jesus was rejected by the city, so His followers can expect similar antagonism. We are called to the city but will not be received gladly. What motivates us is the assurance that there is a new city coming. It is to this hope that we are to bear witness in these seemingly powerful cities that in reality will not endure.

A Tale of Two Cities

The final chapters of the Bible contain a 'tale of two cities' and reveal the outcome of the recovery plan we have been looking at. There we find Babylon the Great, the final manifestation of the city as the place of sin, rebellion and demonic activity. But we also find there the New Jerusalem, the shining city of God, beautiful beyond description and full of the glory of God.

It was Babylon in the Old Testament that moved against

Jerusalem, destroyed it and ransacked its treasures. At the end of the age these two cities will again be the protagonists, symbolically if not historically, but now the outcome is different. It will be Babylon which is destroyed and Jerusalem into which the treasures of the nations will be gathered.[4]

The city is a very important theme in Revelation. Two whole chapters are concerned with Babylon and its fall; a further chapter and a half describe New Jerusalem. These chapters are the climax to the book. The destruction of Babylon is the final act before the return of Christ. The first time 'Hallelujah' is used in the New Testament is when Babylon falls.[5] The New Jerusalem is the place of God's triumph and our inheritance.

This central position of the city should not surprise us now. The city is the concentration of all that the Bible describes as 'the world'. It is the power base for hostile supernatural forces. Babylon the Great has world-wide significance: when Babylon is struck all cities feel the impact:

> *'the great city split into three parts, and the cities of the nations collapsed.'* (Revelation 16:19)

When the city falls, the whole world lies open. 'Hallelujah' is sounded over the fall of Babylon because it is clear now that the battle has been won and no significant opposition remains.

There is too much material in these chapters to examine in detail here, but it is well worth the study. Babylon is made up of the worst features of all cities – the gross affluence of Tyre, the aggression of Nineveh, the sexual sin of Sodom, the occult practices of Old Testament Babylon. The 'Great' in her title is so ironic: this is a haunted city, an urban nightmare, ripe for judgement.

But it is still a city that is in a sense like any other. Music and culture, weddings and celebrations will continue to the end.[6] Most people will be quite unaware of its degenerate state. Babylon is not radically different from our city. We cannot detach ourselves from this awful vision and relegate it to a distant time and place. Babylon is our city at the point of destruction.

Babylon is described as a prostitute. Why? Because she

makes many promises to attract men to her but they find their
deepest needs are not satisfied? Because her glamour and
seductiveness hide the squalor and misery of urban life?
Because she offers herself to be possessed and taken advantage
of but at a price? The image is not explained but it is a poignant
one, and a sharp contrast with the New Jerusalem, the bride of
the Lamb.

Such a city cannot remain. This time it is not just a tower that
reached towards the heavens that prompted God to act: in this
city *'her sins are piled up to heaven'* (Revelation 18:5) and God
at last says 'Enough.' Various catastrophes are mentioned: a
great earthquake, plague, famine, fire and smoke. Clearly the
city's downfall will be very sudden – three times we read that it
is accomplished *'in one hour'*.[7] But is the city destroyed simply
by divine intervention?

At first glance this looks to be the case, but there is another
aspect to Babylon's end.

> *'The beast and the ten horns you saw will hate the prostitute.*
> *They will bring her to ruin and leave her naked; they will eat*
> *her flesh and burn her with fire. For God has put it into their*
> *hearts to accomplish his purpose.'*   (Revelation 17:16–17)

At the very end of history men and women will turn against the
city and the human race will destroy the city. The urban dream
is over, and the scene is set for the final acts of God in this age
and the unveiling of His new home for redeemed humanity, the
New Jerusalem.

No attempt to analyse the vision John saw will do justice to it.
His description points to something breath-taking and awe-
inspiring. God has taken something so debased and corrupted
and transformed it into something so glorious. The story of the
city is one of the most wonderful demonstrations of grace in the
whole Bible. For New Jerusalem is still recognisably a city, with
walls, gates, foundations and at least one main street. For
centuries men and women have been trying to produce a city
that will meet their needs but now the city of God comes down
from heaven, perfect from day one, as a gift for the human race.
Excluded are

> *'the dogs, those who practise magic arts, the sexually immoral, the murderers, the idolaters and everyone who loves and practises falsehood.'*   (Revelation 22:15)

Comparing the list with the 'sins of the city'[8] it is obvious that the city has been purged of all that corrupted and distorted it, so that all its potential for good can be used in the New Jerusalem.

The fact that New Jerusalem is recognisably a city warns us against adopting an unbiblically negative view of our cities; the purging of the city's sins prevents us from holding unrealistic expectations for city life in this age. We need to recognise within our cities the signs of both Babylon the Great and the New Jerusalem if we are to see the city as God sees it.

The wandering of the human race is over. The city has been separated from the spiritual power which oppresses it and is now a true home for men and women. It has been filled with the presence of God in a way that has not been experienced since God walked with Adam in the garden in the cool of the day.

New Jerusalem is in fact a garden city, a beautiful harmony of the urban and the rural. Both city and countryside will be represented in God's future, as the Old Testament prophets had predicted. There is no going back to some rural paradise – as most other religions yearn to do. We look forward to a city, but this city will contain the heart of Eden within its walls. The tree of life is here, having disappeared from view at the Fall, and from the throne of God flows the river of the water of life.[9]

This urban eschatology is important for urban mission. It is a powerful incentive not to abandon the city. Our work and testimony in the city are not insignificant.

> 'The signposts and placards of the eternal city must be erected in our finite cities. God's judgement and promise must be testified to in the city.[10]

We are not faced with 'No Through Road' signs pointing us back to a rural past; we are setting up signposts pointing to the coming city of God. Far from being a form of escapism this urban vision inspires and empowers us to fulfil our urban mandate.

It was with this vision of the city that the Early Church infiltrated the cities of the Roman Empire. Realistic about the city's sins, refusing to be fully identified with it because of their heavenly citizenship, but deeply committed to reaching the cities with the gospel, their strategy was clear. They were known as the people who had turned the world upside down – and it was in the cities, and among the poor in those cities, that this victory was achieved.

PART III

Strategies for the City

Chapter 7

Mission to the City

An Urban World

Centuries ago Isaiah prophesied that ambitious people would *'cover the earth with their cities'* (Isaiah 14:21): in our generation this is being fulfilled in a way previous generations could not have imagined. Already almost fifty per cent of the world's population lives in urban areas and this is rising rapidly.

In 1800, only about five per cent of people lived in cities. A century later this had risen to about fifteen per cent. By 1950 about twenty-eight per cent lived in cities, but just twenty-five years later this had grown to forty-one per cent. It is estimated that by the year 2050 almost eighty per cent of the world will live in urban areas. The rate of urbanisation is hard to visualise. Harvie Conn has written:

> 'the world spawns virtually a new Chicago every month or so.'[1]

This growth is not spread evenly across the world. For the past 200 years most major cities have been in the Western hemisphere, but there is now phenomenal growth in the cities of Asia, Africa, and Latin America. The numbers involved are staggering.

In Latin America there are more than eleven million new city dwellers every year. Sâo Paulo alone is growing by half a million people a year and is likely to have over twenty-eight million inhabitants by the year 2020. Mexico City will probably have over thirty-five million by that date and already half of its population of nearly twenty million is under thirteen years of age.

In Asia the present growth rate will produce by the year 2000 at least fourteen cities with a population of over ten million, thirty-two cities with over five million citizens and more than a hundred with over a million inhabitants. Until 200 years ago Asia had more city dwellers than anywhere else in the world: if present trends continue it will be in this position again by the year 2000. Jakarta is growing at the rate of half a million inhabitants a year and is expected to rocket to twenty-two million by 2020. Shanghai is projected to have nearly thirty-five million people by then.

African cities are smaller at present, but Africa has the fastest urban growth rate in the world. In 1980 only a quarter of Africans lived in the cities, but the situation is changing rapidly. Lagos is expected to increase from about five million in 1985 to over seventeen million in 2020; Cairo may by then have exceeded eighteen million.

In the West, where urbanisation has been proceeding for longer and where the percentage of the city dwellers is higher (over eighty per cent in Australia, sixty-three per cent in Europe and seventy-five per cent in North America), many cities are actually declining for various reasons, such as social migration, alterations to the housing stock and new forms of work. In many places however this is counter-balanced by urban sprawl and the erosion of the green belt. The city may be less densely populated but it extends further than ever.

This does not mean however that cities are becoming less important in the West. As those with resources and mobility move out, the plight of those left in the inner city becomes increasingly serious. Compassion and justice require a Christian response to this. Nor has the city lost its influence. Urbanisation is a process as much as it is physical growth in the size of cities.

'The city is still the social and technological laboratory of the world, even though Western cities are now in dispersion.'[2]

The decisions made, the trends started, the goods marketed, the beliefs promoted in the city will spread throughout society.

For the Church and its mission this presents a stark choice – if it abandons the cities it will be pushed to the edge of society and find itself with no voice and no credibility; if it returns to its biblical roots and targets the cities it can turn the world upside down as the Early Church did. According to the Bible the city has always been crucial – now we can see the evidence before our eyes. However doctrinally sound, evangelistically active, charismatically renewed or socially radical the Church is in the suburbs and small towns, if it does not establish its presence as salt and light in the cities it will not cut much ice. We live in an urban world, but only about nine per cent of evangelicals live in cities of a million or more inhabitants.

It is vital then, that urban mission is given a very high priority, by churches, Christian organisations and mission agencies. In the West, where as we shall see shortly the growth of the cities has frequently found the Church unprepared, this means recognising that areas of the city where the Church is weak are mission fields. They are not to be left to the tiny groups of Christians there but acknowledged as the responsibility of the wider Church. There has been a failure to think and act strategically because we have assumed the West is evangelised. We need to train and send missionaries into our cities.

In Asia, Africa and Latin America, rapid urbanisation has found the Church there as unprepared as were Western churches in previous generations. This is not surprising given the history of missions with the great majority of missionaries working in rural areas. Their ministry was often fruitful, sometimes heroic, but the failure to engage in urban mission laid a very inadequate foundation for the Church's ministry in these urbanising continents. The doughnut picture used earlier needs to be inverted for many of these cities, with most Christians living in the comfortable inner zones rather than in the sprawling shanty towns and slums on the fringes of the cities. But the effect is the same. There are some signs of hope, especially in Latin America, from the Base Ecclesial Communities in Brazil to the burgeoning Pentecostal churches in Santiago, but overall the cities of Asia, Africa and Latin America present a colossal challenge.

'The urban poor constitute the largest unclaimed frontier Christian mission has ever encountered.'[3]

It is important however to clarify the nature of this challenge. Too often cities, especially the inner cities, are discussed in terms of problems but there are also tremendous opportunities, some unique to the cities.

First, there is the sheer number of people in the city. Although the population density produces social and environmental problems and may seem oppressive, the city is a huge harvest field if we are able to see it with the eyes of Jesus.

'When he saw the crowds, he had compassion on them, because they were harassed and helpless, like sheep without a shepherd.' (Matthew 9:36).

It is in the cities that the crowds are to be found. Here there are many who are rootless and lacking in direction, crying out for the compassionate ministry of the Church.

Second, there is the variety of people in the city. Most large cities are amazingly cosmopolitan, some containing one or two large ethnic groups, others with a multi-cultural mix. Los Angeles is a wonderful example of this: it is the second largest Chinese city outside Asia, the second largest Japanese city outside Japan and the second largest Hispanic city in the Western hemisphere, as well as being known as the Vietnamese capital of America. New York contains more Dominicans than anywhere except Santo Domingo and more Haitians than any city except Port-au-Prince.

Urban mission is usually cross-cultural and often affords opportunities to reach people who are unreachable in their own countries. For many years Christians have made special efforts to reach foreign students who are likely to return home to influential postions. But far more resources are needed for ministry among poorer but more settled ethnic communities. One sign of hope in some urban areas is the emergence of ethnic churches who are reaching into their own communities, taking over redundant church buildings and bringing good news into areas where for years the Church has been declining. It is estimated that a new ethnic church begins every week in East London alone. It is in these cosmopolitan cities that the Church has marvellous opportunities to work out the implications of its calling to be a multi-cultural community – opportunities which are not always grasped but which are available in ways that are beyond the reach of churches in monocultural areas.

Third, the cities are where many poor and powerless people live. Biblically the poor are a priority for the Church and there are grounds for expecting God to work significantly among the poor if only the Church is prepared to get involved. Although in many nations the churches are identified with the middle classes and have been unsuccessful in reaching the poor, in areas where really rapid church growth is taking place it is among the poor. The history of revivals suggests that when the Holy Spirit moves in great power there is a mighty harvest among the poor. Targeting the inner cities in the West and the shanty towns elsewhere is crucial if the Church is to fulfil its mandate to the poor and experience the growth that the Lord of the Harvest longs to give.

Fourth, as we have already noted, the cities are places of great influence and centres of communication. Strategically it makes sense to focus on the cities if we want to reach the world. As well as reaching into the inner cities the Church will need to look for access among the powerful in the city centres, but in doing this it must take care to avoid two traps: compromising its radical stance for the sake of increased acceptance, and becoming identified with the rich and powerful in a way that undercuts the gospel.

Thus, whether we look into the Bible or out towards our urban world, we find that we cannot avoid the city and its pivotal importance in God's mission to the nations. But what do we find when we look at the Church and its allocation of personnel and resources? In New Testament times urban mission was a top priority: why is it given such low priority and so few resources today? A brief survey of urban mission in European church history may help us understand how we have reached the present position.

The City in Church History

By the end of the New Testament era the Church was quite firmly established in most of the main cities of the Roman Empire. From these centres the churches were reaching out to neighbouring towns and villages. As numbers increased and administrative developments were necessary, urban bishops were recognised as regional church leaders with responsibility for a city and its environs. Distinct rural churches probably emerged only in the third century, at first in northern Italy and then in France.

When Christianity became the official religion of the Empire this emphasis on the city as the basic church unit continued:

> 'the principle of one parish per city was soon confirmed by legislation; the Council of Chalcedon even made the creation of a new parish conditional upon the unit of a city.'[4]

The church leaders in the larger cities began to take precedence over others and metropolitan bishops exercised wide influence. The recognition of the leader of the church in Rome as the primary church leader was a logical further step down this road.

There are several unhealthy and unbiblical elements here – the emergence of a hierarchical leadership structure, the disastrous partnership of Church and State, and the replacement of trans-local apostolic teams and local elders with static but powerful bishops. But the central importance of the city was clear and the strength of the Church in these strategic centres was a key factor in its growth and influence. Augustine was on firm biblical ground in using the city for his model of the Church in his classic, *The City of God*.

Even as he was writing, however, enormous changes were taking place. Barbarian tribes were making inroads into the Empire and before long Rome itself had fallen. For the next several centuries the cities were in decline, their populations shrank and there was a return to mainly rural life. The Church was faced with the problem of adjusting to this less urban situation – the reverse of the challenge facing it today. The rise of Islam and its capture of the cities of Asia Minor and North Africa, which had been strong Christian centres, increased the problem.

How did the Church adapt in this turbulent period? Sadly, the predominant feature was withdrawal.

> 'The major adaptation made by the church to its new situation was the monastic system ... the withdrawal of the major strength of Christianity from the cities into monasteries, with more of an inward focus than an outward ministry, helped the church to survive a chaotic period in the history of Europe, but it also left the church ill-prepared for the new urban challenge that would come with the revival of cities in later centuries.'[5]

The growth of the Church during the Dark Ages and early Middle Ages (roughly a thousand years – half the history of the Church so far) was negligible. As Ray Bakke notes:

> 'the focus of Christianity was radically shifted from urban centres of North Africa to rural Europe. For one thousand years there was no real gain in the numerical strength of Chritianity. There was simply a swapping of urban real estate for rural real estate.'[6]

No significant attempts were made to engage in mission beyond Christendom where the major cities were at this time.

Cities began to grow again towards the end of the Middle Ages as Europe settled down into a period of relative peace and prosperity. The Church was faced with a new challenge – how to respond to an urbanising society after a millennium of withdrawal. Much of its attention, unfortunately, had been diverted and its energies sapped by the Crusades and their misguided attempts to recapture by force of arms one particular city. There does not seem to have been any clear strategy for the emerging cities. Huge cathedrals were built in the cities but, as with most of today's ecclesiastical buildings, these were empty symbols of the Church in the city. A more positive development was the creation of new religious orders, the Friars, who were usually based in or near cities and who were responsible for much caring ministry there. But overall the Church failed to establish itself decisively in the cities as it had done in the

Roman Empire. It continued to adopt a basically rural model of ministry which was inappropriate to the growing cities of Europe.

The Reformation marked a new stage in various ways, and it is interesting that many of the Reformers were city-based and tried to use the city as the basic unit for their new ecclesiastical organisation. The most familiar example is Calvin's attempt to create a theocratic system in Geneva, which would bind the Church and the city together. A similar but different experiment was the disastrous attempt to set up an Anabaptist kingdom in the city of Münster. Neither provides us with a helpful model of Christian urban ministry for both perpetuated the close allegiance of Church and State that had blighted Europe for centuries. But both recognised the importance of cities for the growth of the Church.

A more helpful example from this period, and one which is much more faithful to the pattern of the Early Church, is the urban ministry of the mainstream Anabaptist (who dissociated themselves from the Münster incident). Until forced out by vicious persecution, their missionaries targeted the main cities of their day in a way that was reminiscent of the apostle Paul.

The rapid urbanisation which accompanied the Industrial Revolution in Europe in the late eighteenth and early nineteenth centuries was the next major challenge to the Church's urban strategy – or lack of strategy. Once again the Church was ill-prepared for this development and failed to establish itself in the growing cities. The urban poor and the working classes in particular became very largely isolated from the churches. From the middle of the nineteenth century until the early twentieth century various attempts were made to reach the cities, money was poured in, missions were built and missioners employed. But it was largely a case of too little too late and in the wrong way.

It seems that for most of the last 1600 years there has been little understanding of biblical teaching on the city and no coherent strategy for urban mission. For much of the time the Church has been on the retreat from the cities, either because the cities themselves were declining or because the Church was ill-equipped to penetrate them in times of expansion. With few exceptions, when the Church did focus its attention on the cities, it became so identified with the city and its power structures as to lose its way and compromise its mission.

Neither withdrawal from the city nor identification with the city will do. If the Church is to make an impact in the city once more a different approach is needed – not a new approach but a recovery of the biblical view of the city and the urban vision and strategy of the New Testament Church.

In the previous section we explored the outlines of a 'theology of the city' which could undergird urban ministry. In the chapters that follow we will return to the biblical story and look in greater detail at a number of characters who in some way ministered to cities. What was their strategy? Are there lessons we can learn from them? As before, the main focus will be on the biblical text itself in order to discover principles for urban ministry today. The contemporary applications are deliberately limited in scope and are intended simply as examples. Cities are complex and varied. Creativity and flexibility are required to develop effective strategies for urban mission and ministry. The examples in the following chapters will relate mainly to Western cities. The same basic principles apply elsewhere but attempting to give examples for cities in Africa, Asia and Latin America is beyond the scope of this book and the experience of the author.

Furthermore, the examples will relate mainly to mission in the inner city for reasons already indicated: the biblical priority given to the poor, the dearth of Christian involvement in these areas, God's tendency to use a bottom-up approach, and my own personal experience in the inner city.

As we explore these biblical characters and strategies we do so in the conviction that urban mission is God's idea. We are not twisting His arm when we come to Him with a concern for the city, for His arms are already stretched out, both towards the city in love and mercy and towards the Church inviting us to join Him in His urban mission.

Chapter 8

Prayer: Abraham and Sodom

*'Then Abraham approached Him and said: "Will you sweep
away the righteous with the wicked? What if there are fifty
righteous people in the city? Will you really sweep it away
and not spare the place for the sake of the fifty righteous
people in it?..." The Lord said. "If I find fifty righteous
people in the city of Sodom, I will spare the whole place for
their sake."'*   (Genesis 18:23–26)

Abraham did not live in a city. He was a nomadic herdsman
who lived in a tent. But he did have an urban vision: he was
looking forward to the establishing of the city of God (Hebrews
11:10). Where he received this revelation we are not told, but
Abraham is the first person in the Bible to exercise any form of
urban ministry. His only human connection with a city was that
his nephew, Lot, lived in Sodom. His urban vision did not lead
him to make his home in the city, but it did result in this prayer
ministry towards the city of Sodom. Abraham is a model for
urban ministry at a distance. Christians in the suburbs and rural
areas can share with urban Christians in ministry towards the
city.

What was it that spurred Abraham to pray? His starting point
was a message from two angel visitors that the cities of Sodom
and Gomorrah were facing judgement. Their sin was so
grievous that God was on the point of intervening (Genesis
18:20–21). Abraham had a personal reason for wanting the city
to be spared, but Lot and his family are not mentioned in this

prayer. Abraham's prayer is for the city as a whole, pleading that it will not be swept away in judgement if there are only a handful of righteous citizens there.

His prayer has been called a 'prayer of negotiation.'[1] From fifty down to just ten Abraham slowly reduces the number of righteous people needed for the city to be spared. Beyond this he does not go but returns home satisfied that the Lord has heard his prayer and will act justly. God has promised that for the sake of ten righteous citizens he will spare the city (Genesis 18:32–33).

What is it that will stir the Church today to pray for the city? It may be that like Abraham one particular city wins our compassion, a city about which God Himself speaks to us. Centuries later Nehemiah was stirred to fast and pray for Jerusalem by a report brought to him by some relatives (Nehemiah 1:1–4). Daniel was studying the Scriptures and was moved by what he read to pray,

> *'Give ear, O God, and hear; open your eyes and see the desolation of the city that bears your Name.'* (Daniel 9:18)

For Jesus it was the sight of Jerusalem in the distance that caused him to weep over it.

Our source of information does not matter. It may be personal experience of living in the city, conversations with others, reports in the media, words of prophecy, understanding what the Bible says about the city or reading books about the city. But effective intercession begins when we see the city as God does. God loves cities and is looking for those with whom he can share His concern for them – those who will weep over them as Jesus and Nehemiah did, who will pray for them as Abraham and Daniel did. Christians living outside the city can be involved in prayerful urban ministry if they are willing to discover God's purpose for the city and commit themselves to this.

How to Pray for the City

Abraham prayed for both justice and mercy – he longed for the city to be spared but he also wanted God to act justly. He does not ask God to spare the city if there is no just reason for doing so; he acknowledges the wickedness there. His prayer demonstrates the biblical balance we have seen in its treatment of the city as a fallen institution but capable of redemption. Whether we are praying for the city centres where decisions are made or for the inner cities where most feel so powerless, our prayers need a similar blend of mercy and justice. We want God to spare the city, but we also want to see it purged and purified, humanised and renewed.

If we are to pray for the city we need information – especially if we do not live in the city ourselves; otherwise our praying will be at best vague and at worst distorted. My perception, shared by many urban church leaders,[2] is that most Christians do not have much idea of what life is really like in the inner city (I suspect the same is true of those who do not work in the city centre but want to pray for it). How can we get such information into the churches?

The obvious way is to contact urban churches and ask for it. We were encouraged by the faithful praying of a group of prayer partners scattered across this country and abroad, to whom we regularly sent information. Some of them prayed for us for over a decade. Short-term missions or other visits can both inform and be a powerful stimulus to prayer. Some of our prayer partners originally came to us as students on a mission team: most have not continued to live in the city but several have gone away radically changed and with a long-term interest. Christians who move out of the city can also help educate and inform their new friends about life there.

A more structured way of receiving information and providing prayer support is by 'twinning'. An urban church is linked with a suburban or rural church in fellowship and mutual service. There are dangers here, particularly if the urban church is patronised or not enabled to contribute its own insights and gifts, but if sensitively handled this arrangement has great potential for all concerned.

Alongside information we need insight if we are to pray effectively. Abraham had God's perspective on Sodom and we need to know how He sees our city. Although there are features common to all cities, each has its own characteristics, and part of our praying will involve seeking God about the ways in which our city is antagonistic to His purposes. What is it about the history, structure, relationships and attitudes of our city that gives it a particular character? If we understand what the churches in the city are up against we can pray more effectively for them. And if we can identify the positive aspects of our city we can pray for these to predominate.

How can we discover these things that affect our city for good or ill? In part by observation, analysis and historical research. The city is as it is today because of what happened in the past. Some areas have an atmosphere or lifestyle that is the result of practices prevalent there in previous generations. Those who live in certain areas may exhibit similar needs and similar strengths – both cultural and spiritual. Where cities were bombed in war there may be a legacy of fear or bitterness; where there has been widespread occult practice there may be a fascination with such things and an atmosphere of oppression; in areas with a history of unemployment and poor housing there may be an overwhelming sense of powerlessness. Those who pray for the city and for churches ministering in the city can pray more specifically if they are aware of such features.

Further insight may come as we pray. Through visions, dreams, prophecies and revelations, through the gift of the discerning of spirits, the churches may be given insights into the spiritual forces at work in the city. This has been our experience several times in Tower Hamlets. In one extended prayer meeting someone had a rather revolting picture of a huge lake of blood that covered our borough. As we continued to pray we found ourselves increasingly conscious of the violence our area had experienced. East London was one of the most heavily bombed areas of England in the last war; it has also been the scene of many violent crimes, Jack the Ripper being only the most notorious of many murderers. Other prophecies have reminded us of the more positive aspects of East End life.

Such insights need to be carefully weighed and then used as guidelines for prayer and action. Where insights received in prayer meetings tally with research into the history and sociology of our city, we can pray with increased confidence that we are on the right track. Prayer walks around the city may also help us get the feel of the area and be a practical demonstration of our commitment to the city.[3]

Useful though such information and insights are, however, the most important ingredient of our praying for the city is compassion. Many of the city's needs are glaringly obvious, especially if we base our praying on the way the Bible presents the city to us. I fear the 'paralysis of analysis' that sometimes results from reports and investigations, be they historical, sociological or spiritual. Our mandate is to pray. 'Prayer for the city is a holy war against all the hostile forces that militate against the peace and well-being of the city,' writes Roger Greenway. 'Because we have not prayed, we have not made an impact for Christ in countless areas of urban life.'[4]

Abraham's prayer for Sodom can act as a model for us as we begin to pray for our cities. We are to remind the Lord that there are some in the city who know and serve Him; we are to pray that God will have mercy on the city for the sake of what is good in it; we can plead that the innocent are not swept away in an indiscriminate judgement. It seems that there is a link between the number of 'righteous' people in the city and its preservation, so perhaps we should go on to pray for men and women of goodwill and integrity to remain in the city or to move in from elsewhere; and for growth in the urban churches. How many are needed for our city to be spared? What should our target be when we pray for inner city areas where church-going is under one per cent?

As we pray for numerical growth in the urban churches, we will surely want to pray also for their witness to be clear, distinctive, radical and attractive. As 'cities set on a hill' within the cities of earth, we can pray that they are beacons of light and communities of salty disciples. Urban churches are on the front line in mission: they need and deserve the persistent prayer support of the wider Church.

We may want to pray also for those who have responsibility for inner city communities – local councils, architects and planners, economists and politicians, large employers whose decisions can vitally affect whole communities. Many in such positions of responsibility are overwhelmed by the scale of the problems they face and the paucity of resources. Some are doing their best but are plagued by doctrinaire attitudes, political extremism and vested interests. Others are apathetic, motivated by self-interest, inflexible and unconcerned. All are battling against the spiritual powers that oppress the city and its institutions.

We may find ourselves stirred to pray for peace in the city. Frustration, powerlessness, boredom, racial harassment and many other factors continue to threaten the peace of the city. Psalm 122 may be a helpful model for us:

> 'Pray for the peace of Jerusalem. May those who love you be secure! "May there be peace within your walls and security within your citadels."' (Psalm 122:6–7)

Insert the name of the city you care for in place of Jerusalem. But we need to be clear about the peace we are praying for: not the Pax Romana sort of peace, an enforced peace, order achieved by intimidation, peace without justice, so that the suburbs feel secure. Our praying is for shalom, the wholesome, just, free, hopeful peace with dignity that our cities need. That is the greatest gift we can ask for in our praying for the city.

What Happens When We Pray for the City?

What was the result of Abraham's prayer for Sodom? When he reached 'what if there are ten?' he stopped and left the outcome to the Lord. For Sodom ten was the minimum number required, but Abraham did not know whether there were ten righteous people in Sodom or not. What he did know was that he had no liberty to reduce the number further; he had fulfilled his responsibility and God had promised to act mercifully if there was even a tiny group of righteous people in the city. Is it presumptuous to say that if there had been ten or more Abraham's praying would have made the difference between the city being destroyed or spared? If so, how significant our prayer ministry could be for our cities. The city may seem so vast that an individual's prayers could have no possible effect, but this incident assures us that they can.

But Sodom was not saved. Angels warned Lot to take his family out of the city to escape destruction and then *'the Lord rained down burning sulphur on Sodom and Gomorrah.'* (Genesis 19:24)

The sad fact was that there were not even ten righteous people in Sodom, so the city could not be spared. God had kept His word to Abraham even though his desire for the city to be spared could not be granted. But his praying was not wasted. His plea that the righteous should not be swept away with the wicked was answered in the rescuing of Lot and his family. Indeed the angels tell Lot that they cannot bring destruction on the city until he has left it (Genesis 19:22), so firmly was the Lord committed to His promise to Abraham. The author of Genesis concludes:

> *'So when God destroyed the cities of the plain, he remembered Abraham, and he brought Lot out of the catastrophe that overthrew the cities where Lot had lived.'*
> (Genesis 19:29)

Our praying for the city is to be realistic. The Bible gives us no reason to expect any human city ultimately to be saved. All human cities will one day be destroyed as completely as was Sodom. But cities can be spared – if they have enough righteous inhabitants and if the people of God are praying for mercy. The people of Nineveh heeded Jonah's words, repented and saved their city: a few generations later it was destroyed, but it had had a respite because of the response of an earlier generation. We are responsible for our generation and its cities. It may be true that praying for the city is an exercise in 'damage limitation' – postponing the judgement, protecting the 'righteous', pleading for mercy – but this does not devalue its importance. At times our praying may lead to revival as in Nineveh; at other times at least a Lot is saved. When Jesus foretold the destruction of Jerusalem he did not suggest anyone prayed for its preservation, but He did say,

> *'Pray that your flight will not take place in winter or on the Sabbath.'* (Matthew 24:20)

Even where a city is doomed we can pray for 'damage limitation', that there will not be unnecessary suffering.

It is therefore a solemn thing to read that Jeremiah was told,

> *'do not pray for this people nor offer any plea or petition for them; do not plead with me, for I will not listen to you.'*
> (Jeremiah 7:16)

He had been told earlier (Jeremiah 5:1) to try to find one honest person in the city, with the promise that even if one could be found the city would be forgiven. Ten had been needed for Sodom to be spared; for Jerusalem one would have been enough, so great was God's love for this city. But no one could be found: praying for Jerusalem was useless – there was not even a Lot to rescue.

But until we hear the Lord telling us to stop we have a mandate to pray for the city. At the end of a long prophecy about Jerusalem's sins the prophet Ezekiel writes these words from the heart of God,

> *'I looked for a man among them who would build up the wall and stand before me in the gap on behalf of the land so that I would not have to destroy it, but I found none.'*
> (Ezekiel 22:30)

The Lord is looking for intercessors who will work with Him to rebuild the city, standing in the gaps where few Christians stand. Big as the city is even one intercessor can make a crucial difference. Prayer for the city is the starting point of all urban ministry.

Is Praying All We Can Do?

This chapter is exceptional in that it is concerned with urban ministry from a distance. The other chapters in this section all require those involved to live in the city. But are there other ways that Christians outside the city can minister to it without moving in?

There have certainly been attempts to do this, many of them well-motivated and in some measure effective. Providing finance for ministry in the inner city has been a frequent response; sometimes this has involved erecting church buildings and mission halls. Tower Hamlets still has several such buildings dating from the middle of the last century when Victorian Christians felt they 'ought to do something for the poor'. There were many more which have now been converted into warehouses or demolished, and most of those that remain are poorly attended and unimaginatively used, but they do represent a previous generation's attempt to minister to the city from a distance.

Some have tried to maintain links with urban churches when they move out to the suburbs. Many churches and mission halls have members who live miles away but commute in on Sundays. Sentimental attachment, positions of power and prestige and a real concern not to leave a struggling congregation have all played their part in this.

But we do need to ask some hard questions about these kinds of 'distance ministries'. Finance can be a mixed blessing. There is no doubt that many urban churches struggle to pay the bills, but outside finance is not always the answer. It may meet short-term needs, but it often reinforces the sense of dependency and powelessness in the community. Finance from outside has sometimes come with strings attached or with a patronising attitude, although this is less true recently. More disturbing is the tendency of such finance to shore up churches where the life has departed, rather than initiating mission.

What is the point of maintaining expensive premises when the congregation could meet more comfortably in a living room? The inner city is littered with church buildings which seat hundreds but are attended by a handful. The money that makes this possible comes from external funds, from denominational subsidies or from legacies and trusts. Millions of pounds are wasted in this way that could be invested in strategic mission. Some argue that a 'witness' is maintained. But what sort of a witness is a tiny handful in a huge auditorium? While the buildings remain the Church at large can pretend to be still represented there, but pretence it is, obscuring the real state of the Church in the inner city and hindering true mission there. Who is kidding whom?

What should be done with these buildings? Some should be

demolished or sold for development, as they are quite impractical for any viable congregation. Others should be turned over to thriving churches in need of premises or mission teams with a strategy for the area. One of the hindrances to such radical but sensible action is that the trustees who control these resources often live miles away and have no idea what is really needed in the inner city. Trying to minister to the city from a distance, all they end up doing is squandering resources and hindering effective mission.

As for the continuing involvement in urban churches of those who do not live locally, whatever the motivation such commuting does not in the long run aid urban mission. As with the buildings, it creates a false impression of the strength of urban churches. It inhibits the development of inner city church leaders – for often it is leaders who are commuting – and it prevents radical steps being considered. A survey in 1974 revealed that eighty per cent of Protestant church leaders in Toxteth, Liverpool, lived outside the local area. Quoting this as typical of many inner city areas, Dave Cave comments:

> 'Travelling leadership is one of the main contributors to the death of inner city churches.'[5]

Urban mission is the responsibility of the whole Church, but there are ways not to do it! The only urban ministry that the Bible authorises for those who do not live in the city is to pray for it as Abraham did. Other forms of support – finance, encouragement, provision of refuges or whatever – may be useful but need to be provided in an attitude of service and in response to the demands of a coherent urban strategy. Those who want to do more than this need to consider relocation as their first step.

Chapter 9

Presence: Jeremiah and Babylon

'This is what the Lord Almighty, the God of Israel, says to all those I carried into exile from Jerusalem to Babylon: "Build houses and settle down; plant gardens and eat what they produce. Marry and have sons and daughters; find wives for your sons and give your daughters in marriage, so that they too may have sons and daughters. Increase in number there; do not decrease. Also, seek the peace and prosperity of the city to which I have carried you into exile. Pray to the Lord for it, because if it prospers, you too will prosper."'
(Jeremiah 29:4–7)

The unthinkable had happened; Jerusalem had fallen and all but the poorest inhabitants had been carried off to Babylon. The exiles were confused and homesick. Why had God allowed His city to be destroyed? What was the future now for their nation? Could God still be with them in this alien city? Psalm 137 expresses powerfully the sadness and dislocation they felt:

'How can we sing the song of the Lord while in a foreign land?'
(Psalm 137:4)

Some so-called prophets had raised their hopes that they would soon return home, but were they speaking the truth? What should they plan for? What should they do?

Into their confusion comes this letter from Jeremiah, the one person who had forseen the destruction of Jerusalem. His advice was clear: God has placed you in Babylon; don't expect

83

to escape in the near future; settle down and make your home in the city; get involved in its life and activities; raise families and build community there; get rid of your negative attitudes[1] and seek the city's good.

What relevance does this situation have to contemporary urban mission? Few Christians are in the city as war captives; many have the option of moving out. But it is as true now as it was when Jeremiah wrote and when Abraham prayed that the presence of God's people in the city can make a crucial difference. Prayer for the city can be offered from a distance but many of the answers depend on Christians following Jeremiah's strategy and getting personally involved in city life.

The Church in the inner city has been weakened over many years by two significant trends – the very small number of Christians willing to move into the inner cities and the very large numbers moving out. The ring doughnut picture used earlier is not static: suburban churches are still growing at the expense of the churches in the inner city. Urban people are being converted but many of them move out, drawn by the prevailing middle-class ethos of the Church into middle-class areas. Sociologists call this 'redemption and lift': it has positive features but it decimates urban churches. Two strategic changes are needed – Christians living in the inner city need to settle down there and Christians elsewhere need to relocate to the inner city.

Stay in the City

I do not believe that every Christian living in the inner city must stay there for life, but I do believe that no Christian should move without a clear call of God. It is not wrong to consider the advantages of living elsewhere, but it is tragic that 'while God can be seen moving *towards* the city, God's people move in the opposite direction.' The temptation to move out is great, but if we are serious about 'seeking first God's kingdom' we will want to look beyond our own interests to the wider issues. Several years ago David Sheppard wrote *Bias to the Poor*; most of the poor in question live in our inner cities, so this, together with what the Bible says about the strategic importance of the cities, should lead us to a 'bias to the city' position. While it is possible God may call Christians out of the city, our expectation is that He wants them to stay and serve Him there. This bias is not decisive: it can be overcome by clear guidance elsewhere, but it will act as a check, helping some to resist the 'flight to the suburbs'.

Christians are in the inner city for various reasons. Some, like my sons, were born and raised there and had no choice in the matter; others have moved in to study or work locally; a small but growing number have moved in as a response to God's call to urban mission. None are immune from the temptation to move out. The exiles in Babylon were not there by choice, but God's word to them was 'I put you there.' This is the place to start. However you got to the inner city, God has placed you there – stay there until He tells you to move. Settle down, stop wanting to leave, commit yourself to God's urban mission.

We had several people come to Tower Hamlets to study or work with no intention of staying there, but God spoke to them about settling down. For some this has been costly and not without tears, but their decision to stay has brought great joy and has strengthened urban churches.

Centuries ago the author of the Letter to Diognetus wrote:

'As the soul is to the body, so are Christians to their city.'

Jesus told His disciples, who would have preferred to be in rural Galilee, to *'stay in the city'* until the Spirit came in power. The challenge to urban Christians is to stay in the city, bearing witness there in word and deed, believing that in time God's Spirit will bring renewal, even revival to the city.

Go into the City

Jeremiah urged the exiles to *'increase in number there'* (Jeremiah 29:6). Their present strength was not enough. In the same way today it is not enough that fewer Christians move out of the city; many areas are almost devoid of Christian witness. A more radical change is needed if the presence of God's people in the city is to become adequate for the task of urban mission. Strategic relocation is necessary.

There are three ways in which churches can grow: biologically, as members have children and nurture them in the faith; through conversion; and by transfer as Christians move from one area or church to another. There has been a tendency to discount the third method because it produces no net gain – shunting Christians around is not church growth. This is true, of course, but it neglects the strategic value of such Christians and their potential mission. Ten suburban Christians transferring from a large church into a small inner city church produces no net gain in itself, but it may make a very great difference to the mission of the churches involved, with the result that real growth takes place in both.

Inner city Christians are responsible for biological and conversion growth in urban areas, but responsibility for transfer growth rests largely with churches elsewhere. I believe a significant relocation of personnel is needed for urban mission. Some time ago I was talking with the leader of one of the largest churches in this country, who asked what his 1000+ member church in one of the wealthiest parts of England could contribute to urban mission. My reply was a single word – people. I am convinced that people – not money, buildings, experts or programmes – are the key. If God's mission to the city is to be fulfilled, the people of God will need to be mobilised.

But this will involve churches giving away their members! It will mean city centre churches encouraging members who live in the inner city to stop commuting to church and worship locally. Nobody really benefits from this situation: local churches are deprived of vital personnel and commuter Christians warm pews elsewhere but are not stretched or developed in any way. I have written to the leaders of some city-centre churches about this; I received one very gracious and positive response but none of the others even deigned to reply. It is vital the large central churches begin to develop a sense of responsibility for the inner city around them.

It will also mean suburban churches challenging members to move into the inner city, courageously swimming against the tide and making costly decisions. And let's be clear that the inner city does not need the cast-offs from suburban churches – it needs leaders, the mature and gifted members, the ones who will really leave a gap. It needs those able to cope with cross-cultural mission, those willing to serve rather than expecting to take over.

Why should churches outside the inner city even consider such radical and uncomfortable possibilities?

First, it is time the Church seriously regarded the inner cities as a mission field. We will need to stop pretending we live in a Christian nation and develop a pioneer mission strategy for our cities, training and releasing personnel for this. Fifteen years ago I was commissioned by a suburban church in north east London as a missionary to Tower Hamlets. I could drive to this church from Tower Hamlets in twenty-five minutes but I was regarded as a missionary in the same way as others the church had sent to India or Africa. If suburban and provincial churches learn to see inner cities as mission fields, they may be prepared to release their members.

Second, it is time suburban churches repaid their debt to inner city churches. Eddie Gibbs, an expert on church growth, writes:

> 'Frequently the inner city church loses many of its young families as they improve their financial position to the point where they are able to move out to the better housing and social amenities of suburbia. The churches located in favoured suburbia will, therefore, grow through the transfer of such church families.'[2]

Many people have been converted in the cities: urban churches are not small because of few conversions, but because most of their converts move to the suburbs.

Third, it is time the Church took seriously the call to equalise resources. Paul wrote:

> *'Our desire is not that others might be relieved while you are hard pressed, but that there might be equality.'*
>
> (2 Corinthians 8:13)

He was writing about finance but the same principle applies to personnel. Provincial and suburban churches have relatively large staffs and many able volunteers; inner city churches have fewer staff and less able volunteers, even though pastoral needs are vastly greater. Justice rather than charity requires a strategic change.

Fourth, it is time for the resources of larger churches to be released. Far too many Christians sit comfortably in suburban churches, attending meetings, reading their Bible, tithing their income, exercising their spiritual gifts and doing polite Christian things. We talk about the kingdom of God advancing but we are way behind the front-line. For salt to be effective it must be evenly distributed. Leaders in large provincial churches have told me they do not have enough jobs to go round. People who could be highly significant in urban mission are given the offering to count! Such squandering of resources benefits nobody except the enemy of the Church who continues to dominate our cities.

How can such a release of personnel take place? It will not happen overnight; a lot of groundwork needs to be done – teaching a theology of the city in the churches, developing a prayer concern for the cities, expanding our familiar individualistic models of guidance so that people stop asking, 'Lord, where in suburbia do you want me to live?', breaking down the barriers of ignorance and fear that hinder Christians from considering moving into the inner city. Leaders will need to lead by example, and they will be criticised for doing so. There are many practical issues to weigh up that I am not attempting to address. But strategic relocation is crucial for urban mission.

Jesus told Paul, *'get up and go into the city'* (Acts 9:6). I believe He is calling for His disciples today to do the same. The presence of increasing numbers of God's people in the city is vital for its preservation. Without this none of the other strategies we will be looking at are feasible.

Seek the Shalom of the City

It was not enough for the exiles to live in Babylon: they had no choice about this. What was important was how they participated in the life of that city. Jeremiah urges them to get fully involved in its economic and social life; to raise their families there and to plan for future generations still living in the city. They were also to pray for the city – for, not against it – aware that their destiny was caught up with Babylon's. Their goal was to seek the shalom of the city.

Christians in the inner city (and the city centre) are called to a similar level of involvement. It is not enough to live there or even to evangelise there. Shalom is a rich concept that requires a commitment to the total well-being of the community. Although our ultimate citizenship is in heaven and thus we retain a degree of separation from what the city stands for, seeking shalom in the city will only happen as the Church becomes identified with the needs, concerns and aspirations of local people. Urban mission has been hindered by a long standing 'us/them' divide, with the Church seen as an alien, middle-class institution, 'not for the likes of us'.

Seeking shalom in the city will call for us to be involved in caring ministry towards the many hurting, lonely, marginalised people who live there. Many urban churches have concentrated on this aspect of shalom. Perhaps more than anywhere else there has been a recognition that saving souls and caring for bodies and minds cannot be divorced without doing violence to the gospel.

There are dangers here, however, Some churches have hidden behind such ministries and failed to proclaim the gospel. Some have been guilty of bribery, requiring people to sit through a gospel message to receive a bun and soup at the end. Some of the caring that goes on increases dependency rather than equipping people for life. It is important too that urban churches do not neglect the ordinary urban families who are not so obviously needy but who are more numerous than the destitute; if we do this it communicates the message once more that the Church is not for them – it is run by do-gooders for down-and-outs. Many urban people would not be seen dead in a mission hall. Caring must be part of a broader strategy if it is to lead towards shalom.

Another aspect of this is the call to work for structural changes that will increase peace and justice in the city. The Church in the city has a long history of caring for casualties and in a fallen society these will never be absent. But there is scope also for working towards changes in the systems that cause or exacerbate such casualties. Otherwise, as cities deteriorate and caring agencies are stretched beyond breaking point by the growing number of wounded, alienated and suffering people, the prospects are bleak. This is part of the Church's ministry also, albeit a complicated and difficult part, if it is truly seeking the shalom of the city.

The exiles were also called to be spiritually involved in the city, to pray for its shalom. Christians in the city can join with intercessors elsewhere in praying as Abraham did for God to have mercy upon the city. We are to pray for its prosperity – not the typical urban prosperity which is achieved through injustice and oppression and which produces glaring inequalities between the rich and the poor, the suburbs and the inner city. Our prayer is for a more just distribution of opportunities and resources in the city for the good of all its citizens.

Daniel in Babylon

What about political involvement in the city? Is this part of the Church's mandate to see shalom? Some would argue that such involvement is essential in order to influence the city for good. Others would doubt the wisdom or effectiveness of this and urge Christians to concentrate on other strategies. My own view is that socio-political activity is a valid ministry for urban Christians but that it is neither the place to start nor the final solution. The first priority in places where the Church is so weak in numbers and so low in morale is to produce growing, envisioned and indigenous churches. Energies that might be put into political activities should be devoted to this first, or else there will not be the personnel or credibility for local churches to maintain such initiatives. Where this is achieved, I do see some valid political ministries developing (politics after all, literally means 'affairs of the city' the *polis*).

At least one of the exiles in Babylon was involved in politics. Provided we remember that Babylon was far from being a democracy, Daniel's life can provide us with some useful insights in this area. Probably a teenager from a noble family, Daniel's name was changed, he was thoroughly re-educated and he was expected to enter fully into Babylonian culture. His firm but gracious refusal to compromise his standards or deny his faith won him respect and at the end of his training he was given an influential position among the king's advisors (Daniel 1).

His career was almost ended by the king's threat to all of his counsellors, but he received divine revelation that enabled him to survive the crisis (Daniel 2), His next task was to warn the king against arrogance and oppressing the poor. *'Is not this the great Babylon I have built as the royal residence, by mighty power and for the glory of my majesty?'* asked Nebuchadnezzar (Daniel 4:30). The city once more symbolises self-sufficiency and human pride. It was this that provoked God to action, and at the end of his life the king remembered Daniel's words and acknowledged the Lord as God.

Daniel seems to have dropped out of public life after this until summoned to interpret writing on the wall on the last night of the Babylonian Empire. He shows no interest in the reward or power offered – empty indeed on that night – but they were forced on him (Daniel 5). It is quite astonishing to find him still in a key political position under the new king, Darius. An empire had come and gone, a new administration had been formed, but Daniel remained, such was his ability and integrity. In spite of opposition, he continued to be a political influence into the reign of the next king, Cyrus (Daniel 6). His early decision not to compromise had stood him in good stead.

Some important principles can be noted here relevant to any considering involvement in urban politics.

(1) The need for integrity and distinctiveness. Compromised Christian involvement in politics is worse than none at all. The pressure to conform and cut ethical corners is great, as is the temptation to let slip one's church involvement. The integrity required will often cut across party lines, but Daniel demonstrates the possible influence of someone prepared to be true to principle.

(2) The need for ability and wisdom. Daniel was an exceptionally able man, intelligent and discerning. Local government in urban areas is plagued by incompetent administrators and politicians. Eager for power, with an axe to grind, or simply looking for an easy life, such people

clog up the system and the needy are not helped. Well-meaning Christians lacking the necessary skills will not be effective in politics.

(3) The need for divine anointing. Daniel received supernatural wisdom and revelation without which he would have lost both his job and his life. The anointing of the Holy Spirit and His gifts are not just for use in the church; they are vital for those called to serve Christ in the political arena. The words of wisdom and knowledge, the discerning of spirits and the gift of faith would seem to be particularly relevant.

(4) The need to represent the poor and powerless. Daniel took the opportunity to call for social justice and to challenge oppression (Daniel 4:27). This is surely a primary goal for any Christian involved in urban politics – to challenge the rich and powerful, to expose corruption and to champion the down-trodden. This must be accompanied by a firm refusal to seek wealth or status as primary aims; it will also require the courage to put one's own position on the line rather than accept an unjust status quo.

Is such involvement possible? Daniel's experience suggests that it is just possible, but only with supernatural intervention. This is not surprising, for the power behind the city is itself supernatural: to challenge or seek to control that power for good will require supernatural wisdom and grace. Without it there is a danger that the pressure will be too great, leading to Christians abandoning political involvement or, worse still, continuing to be involved but at the cost of compromise, which plays right into the hands of the power of the city.

Another biblical character who found himself in a similar position was Joseph in Egypt. His enlightened economic policy, also prompted by divine revelation, met the needs of thousands of hungry people. A further example is Esther in Susa, who used her influential position to expose a corrupt official, to thwart a violent and racist policy and to protect an endangered ethnic minority. None of these people asked for political influence, but finding themselves with it they retained their integrity and committed themselves to serve God there. These are the relevant models for Christians considering political involvement

– not the kings or politicians of theocratic Israel. Political involvement may be one way of seeking the shalom of the city, but its influence should not be over-estimated nor its difficulties minimised. And it is crucial that the Church, as a community, does not try to wield political power, or else it will find itself ruled by the very powers its task is to expose.

The task of the Church is to be present in the city in increasing numbers, to seek the shalom of the city and to pray for it. This will involve prophetic, evangelistic, pastoral and many other functions, all of which will require the empowering of the Holy Spirit and a very definite conviction that the Lord has brought us to the city to serve Him there. The specific tasks will vary enormously, so urban churches will need to be flexible and imaginative, but the first priority is the release and relocation of personnel, and the establishing of vibrant urban churches.

Chapter 10

Prophecy: Jonah and Nineveh

'The word of the Lord came to Jonah, son of Amittai: "Go to the great city of Nineveh and preach against it, because its wickedness has come up before me." But Jonah ran away from the Lord and headed for Tarshish ... Then the word of the Lord came to Jonah a second time: "Go to the great city of Nineveh and proclaim to it the message I give you." Jonah obeyed the word of the Lord and went to Nineveh ... He proclaimed: "Forty more days and Nineveh will be overturned." The Ninevites believed God ... When God saw what they did and how they turned from their evil ways, he had compassion and did not bring upon them the destruction he had threatened. But Jonah was greatly displeased and became angry.' (Jonah 1:1–3; 3:1–5, 10; 4:1)

The Grumpy Prophet

Jonah did not want to go to Nineveh. Tarshish was about as far in the opposite direction as anyone in the ancient world could have thought of going (probably the area we now know as the Costa Brava). When the Lord eventually managed to persuade him to go, he delivered his message and then waited to see what would happen. As he had suspected, as soon as the Ninevites began to repent God rescinded the threat of judgement and spared the city. Jonah was furious.

How do we interpret the behaviour of this grumpy prophet? Why was he so reluctant to go to Nineveh? To begin with Jonah was a small-town Israelite (from Gath-hepher, near Nazareth): the prospect of prophesying in mighty Nineveh was enough to make anyone quail. His message was not exactly calculated to make him friends there either! But he was not just afraid of the consequences for himself; he was also afraid that there might be a positive response and that the city would be spared. That was the last thing Jonah wanted for the capital city of the oppressive Assyrian nation. Unlike the Lord, Jonah had no desire to see the city spared. He fully agreed with God that it was wicked, but he did not want an urban ministry.

Jonah's reluctance resulting in flight to Tarshish is a biblical example of the trend we looked at in the last chapter. God had a mission to the city but most of His people are moving away from it. God loves the city but many of His servants have written it off; they are happy to condemn its wickedness, but they are not convinced it is worth sparing, nor are they willing to call it to repentance.

Jonah already had a national reputation as a prophet. He was serving the Lord faithfully in his own nation and had brought a significant prophecy to the king (2 Kings 14:25). Many today who are serving the Lord effectively in suburban or provincial settings would no more dream of ministering in the inner city than Jonah wanted to in Nineveh. Where do most Christian leaders live? How many with a national ministry have any involvement in urban areas? Perhaps the relocation of person-nel should start here?

Two chapters, one storm and one whale-journey after he first heard God's call Jonah is back at square one, but this time he obeys, in spite of his attitude to the city. God so cares for the city that He will speak to His reluctant people as often as necessary about it until there is a response. He is prepared to use even grumpy prophets to speak His word to the city. The city seems so large and daunting as to make many feel hopeless and unable to get involved, but the story of Jonah is testimony to the potential of one man's ministry – and a reluctant man at that.

Jonah's message is short, blunt and totally negative, speaking only of destruction. Was this the whole of God's word to Nineveh? Brevity is not a sign that a prophecy is deficient:

Haggai once prophesied, '"*I am with you*," declares the Lord' and stopped there (Haggai 1:13). Indeed much modern-day prophecy would benefit from being shorter rather than longer.

But the spirit of the prophecy seems deficient. We know that God longed to have mercy on the city, but Jonah speaks only of destruction. Indeed we can almost imagine him rubbing his hands together in anticipation! It is not false prophecy, for the message is accurate, but Jonah has not communicated God's heart toward the city. He has expressed God's anger about the city's sin but left out His desire to spare it.

Yet in spite of Jonah's reluctance and bad attitude, in spite of the inadequate message, the city repented and was spared. The response is overwhelming and without parallel in the Old Testament. The grace of God is such that the brusque message of this grumpy prophet produces a city-wide response. God loves the cities of men and women far more than they themselves do.

The response began among ordinary people. The decree of the king (Jonah 3:7) was important in that it represented the official reaction from the city authorities, but it was largely redundant in its effects: the citizens were already doing what was decreed. The outcome that human wisdom would have anticipated – the imprisonment or execution of Jonah, the suppression of popular discontent – never happened. Revival came to Nineveh. The history of revivals in Britain reveals that they usually begin among ordinary people, the urban or rural poor. Revival is from the bottom up rather than from the top down. Paul's experience was that few converts were rich, powerful or academic (1 Corinthians 1:26–31). The present concentration of the Church in the prosperous and powerful sections of society, and the inevitable neglect of urban (and some rural) areas, demonstrate a disturbing lack of strategy, flying in the face of biblical and historical evidence. It may be in urban areas that the conflict is fierce and the Church weak, but it is here that the potential for revival is greatest. If we are to take seriously expectations of revival, we will need to see a renewed commitment to the cities as the key targets. If revival comes to the cities without this we will miss it! If revival comes elsewhere it will not have the impact we are hoping for. The cities are the key.

Bringing God's Word to the City

What does it mean to prophesy in and to the city? How does the Church's prophetic ministry differ from its evangelistic mandate? To whom should the prophets be speaking?

Before looking for hints in Jonah's ministry, it is worth noting that prophecy in various forms is firmly back on the Church's agenda. For some this means a rediscovery of hope as they study the parts of the Bible which speak about the return of Christ and a determination to be part of a Church that is prepared as a bride fit for the Bridegroom. For many this means a conviction that God still speaks to His people through contemporary prophets, to encourage, challenge and comfort them. Although charismatic renewal was dubbed a 'tongues movement' in its early days, prophecy has been a far more significant element. A third strand focuses on the role of the Church as prophesying to the world, calling it to repentance and interpreting the signs of the times. All three expressions have had their aberrations but the recovery of the prophetic dimension of the Church's ministry and the 'prophethood of all believers' is one of the significant features of our generation.

Prophecy is important for urban Christians. Living in a noisy, man-made environment it is vital to hear the voice of God, through the Bible and through prophecy. Surrounded by human wisdom and power structures it is crucial to discover God's perspective on urban issues. But there are aspects of the rediscovery of prophecy that concern me.

One disappointing feature of much eschatology is the lack of attention the city receives. Although this is a major theme of many prophetic Scriptures, not least the final chapters of Revelation, it is given at best cursory treatment. Is this further evidence of the anti-urban bias in the Church? While urban Christians can rejoice in the sense of destiny stirred by those who draw our attention to God's future purposes, this encouragement would be so much greater if the future of the city were given in its biblical place.

As for charismatic prophesying, have you noticed how rural its language is? You enter a world of shepherds and mountains, trees and gardens. There is nothing wrong with this – many biblical prophecies use similar images – but there are not many mountains in the inner city, gardens are for the fortunate few, and shepherds are redundant. Cannot God use urban images to communicate with city Christians? Urban imagery is just as biblical – but perhaps we feel that rural is more spiritual than urban? If prophecy is the 'now' word of God it is also the 'here' word of God, bringing revelation to us in terms we can relate to.

I have been encouraged by examples of urban prophecies in the church in Tower Hamlets (where I have spoken about this). An oily rag being squeezed out as a symbol of the outpouring of the Spirit, plants breaking through paving stones, and the imagery of the building site have been for me much more potent than rivers in the desert and cascading fountains.

But Jonah prophesied to a pagan city, not to the people of God. Much as urban churches need to hear the word of the Lord themselves, how are they to bring it to their cities? The book of Jonah is one of three Old Testament books that are concerned not with Israel but with pagan nations. The other two are Nahum and Obadiah, and several other prophets also prophesied in part to foreign nations or cities.[1] These passages are some of the most neglected parts of the Bible. When did you last hear teaching from them? Only Jonah is familiar – in part because the fish incident makes such a good children's story. But it is these prophecies that are relevant to the Church in a non-Christian society.

One of the concerns I have about some so-called prophetic calls to the nation or analyses of society is that they assume modern nations are analogous to Israel. Passages (like the most familiar 2 Chronicles 7:14) which urge the people of God to repent and seek God so that He will heal their land cannot simply be applied to Britain, the USA, or any other nation. The Church is an international community that has no 'land' of its own. Attempting a prophetic evalutaion of society within this framework shows how conformed we still are to a Christendom mindset. We do have a mandate to pray for our nation and its cities and its rulers, but the biblical basis for this is to be found in these neglected prophecies to pagan nations.

Perhaps it is in the inner cities that this can be seen most clearly. Elsewhere it may still be possible to cling to the illusion that Britain or the USA are Christian nations and that the task of the Church is priestly, representing the views of a believing, though not practising, majority, and where possible pressuring those in authority to enforce such views. But in the inner city, where perhaps one in two hundred attends a church, the emptiness of this position is obvious. The Church is a prophetic minority, not a moral majority.

How then does Jonah help us understand what it means to bring God's word to the city?

First, we need to note that Jonah is not an evangelist. He brings no good news; he asks for no personal response; there is no reason to think the Ninevites came into a relationship with the God they now feared. The city was spared and reformed, but its citizens were not converted. Prophecy and evangelism are closely linked and both are ministries of the Church in the city, but they are distinct.

Second, Jonah is not a social analyst. He sends no commission; he conducts no interviews; he produces no reports. Such things may be useful but they are not prophecy. They may contain prophetic elements, as may evangelism, but prophecy is not to be equated with socio-political comments. Urban life is very complex and any worthwhile analysis will reflect this complexity, but prophecy is essentially simple, cutting through to the heart of the matter. True prophecy comes out of revelation rather than investigation. The prophetic role of the Church in the city is to declare to the city what God thinks of it. Prophecy brings a spiritual and moral word; it uncovers attitudes and motives that hide beneath the surface.

Third, Jonah addresses the city as a whole. Evangelism addresses individuals for cities cannot be saved; prophecy may address individuals but it can also be directed towards the whole city and deal with wider issues in the structures, policies and institutions of the city. One aspect of this is the exposing of the powers at work in the city. When Jesus died, He *'made a public spectacle of them'* (Colossians 2:15). Since then they have been hiding but are still active in the city and elsewhere. Part of the Church's task is to name these powers, to reveal their influence, to unmask their activities. This is both for the Church's own benefit so that it can pray and act in the light of this revelation, and also for the sake of the city, whatever its response.

What is it about our city that most concerns God? Jonah speaks only in general terms of 'wickedness' but Nahum later spells out clearly that Nineveh was characterised by violence, arrogant militarism and economic oppression. What would God put His finger on in our city? It may not be the things we regard as worst or most obvious. Sadly the Church has often 'majored on the minors' and has spoken out about certain types of anti-social behaviour or personal immorality that threaten middle-class security or sensibilities. Or else it has swung to the opposite extreme and been concerned only about some notion of social justice whilst winking at unrighteousness. True prophecy will not be captive to either right-wing or left-wing analyses.

An important aspect of the Church's prophetic role is its unashamed use of the Bible. We cannot assume any prior knowledge of its message, nor should we expect people to respect it. We need not to be offended if it is laughed off as an ancient and irrelevant document, and we have no right to impose it. But we have a responsibility to declare God's word on issues in the city. Ichthus Christian Fellowship leader Roger Forster's reading of Romans 1 to a local council meeting in South East London as part of a Christian protest against the moral stance and social policies of that council is a recent example of this.[2] The city needs to hear the words of the Bible, words that challenge its godless autonomy, whatever its response.

The Church is called not only to pray for the city and to be present there to serve it; it is also to bring God's word to the city. Jonah seems simply to have walked into the heart of Nineveh and prophesied in the open air. We may achieve this using other methods but our calling is the same.

The Sign of Jonah

When Jesus refers to the story of Jonah He speaks not only about his preaching but about the prophet himself being a sign to the Ninevites (Luke 11:30–32). Some have suggested that the gastric juices of the big fish had discoloured him so that his appearance startled them, but the parallel message (Matthew 12:39–41) indicates that it was Jonah's survival and supernatural rescue that was the essence of the sign. Whatever its nature, it is clear that the sign was Jonah himself, not just his message.

The Church in the city is called to be a sign, a prophetic community that models an alternative, that demonstrates what it proclaims. The day of the isolated prophet is over: ever since the incarnation made the word flesh the prophetic ministry has needed a community to speak out from, a community with a shape, ethos and lifestyle that gives integrity to the message of its prophets. The building of such communities, fully a part of their localities yet radically distinct, is a primary task of urban mission.

To be such a sign the Church needs to see the city as God does, to embody His vision for it, and to live in the opposite spirit from the prevailing evil in the city. A church in Sodom, for example, would have been a prophetic community as it practised sexual purity and ministered to the needs of the poor; a church in affluent Tyre would have been a sign by adopting a simple lifestyle; a church in Nineveh would have welcomed slaves and prisoners of war into its fellowship on equal terms and would have refused to participate in aggressive military campaigns.

Churches in contemporary cities will need to seek God for revelation about their cities. In some places the church will need to become a peaceful multi-racial community if it is to speak with integrity to a divided and fearful society. In others the church may need to renounce its large, imposing buildings if it is to stand with the poor and powerless. In some settings there may be one key local issue where the church will need to become involved and model an alternative.

One of the issues in Tower Hamlets which we were involved in for several years was education. In common with many inner city areas schools are under great pressure, morale is low, standards are poor, there is massive under-achievement and spiritual values have little place. We responded in two ways – by actively supporting Christian teachers in local schools, and by starting our own Christian school.[3] This small community school, which is multi-racial, open to all, but with a distinctive Christian ethos and approach, has struggled in various ways but is gaining a good local reputation. Our hope is that it will not only provide a good education for those pupils who attend, but that it will be an alternative model which will have a prophetic contribution to make.

Jonah's message was negative and his attitude was resentful. He didn't want to go to Nineveh and he had nothing good to offer the city, but God acted and the city was spared. The real miracle of the story is not the prophet-swallowing fish but the citywide response to Jonah's preaching. The Church in the city is called to a similar prophetic ministry, but we are not to copy Jonah's attitudes. Our message may be as uncompromising as his, and we will need to speak out against the sins of the city as he did; but we can also offer hope, both in our words and by modelling an alternative lifestyle. The response may have been unusual but the message of the book of Jonah is that one person can exercise an effective urban ministry – how much more prophetic communities planted in the inner cities of our nations and throughout the world's cities?

'Should I not be concerned about that great city?' asks the Lord in the final verse of the book. That question continues to challenge the Church today as it looks out on an urbanised world and cities many times larger than Nineveh.

Chapter 11

Praise: Joshua and Jericho

'Now when Joshua was near Jericho he looked up and saw a man standing in front of him with a drawn sword in his hand. Joshua went up to him and asked, "Are you for us or for our enemies?" "Neither," he replied, "but as commander of the army of the Lord I have now come." Then Joshua fell face down on the ground in reverence and asked him, "What message does my Lord have for his servant?" ... Then the Lord said to Joshua, "See, I have delivered Jericho into your hands" ... Joshua commanded the people, "Shout! For the Lord has given you the city!"'

(Joshua 5:13–14; 6:2, 16)

The Fortress City

Forty years earlier the people of Israel had turned back from the border of the Promised Land, discouraged by the spies' report of the large and fortified cities that awaited them (Numbers 13:28). Now they were back and within sight of one of those cities, the fortress of Jericho. Joshua, who had been one of those spies, knew all about what lay ahead; he knew too that this was the crucial test for the Israelites. If they took Jericho the land lay open before them, but if they failed here they might as well return to the desert. Just as the Lord later brought Jonah back to Ninevah, so he had brought the Israelites back to Jericho.

In our day the Lord seems to be bringing the Church back to face the challenge of the cities, a challenge that went largely

103

unheeded in previous generations. We face the same choice that Joshua was facing as he considered Jericho – will we be put off by the difficulties of tackling the city (some real, some of our own imagining), or will we respond to that challenge? There is no way to avoid the city: if the Church does not engage in urban mission it cannot have more than a marginal influence in society.

The Israelites had learnt many lessons since they were last on the edge of the Land, lessons which would stand them in good stead in the campaign that lay ahead. They were fresh from the miraculous crossing of the Jordan, which they had celebrated by setting up remembrance stones, a testimony to the power of their God. They had consecrated themselves anew to the Lord and all the males had been circumcised. They had been encouraged by the report of the spies sent to Jericho:

> 'The Lord has surely given the whole land into our hands; all the people are melting in fear because of us.'
>
> (Joshua 2:24)

Faith and vision were rising – but still the fortress city stood in their way.

The Church, likewise, has experienced global renewal and learnt much in recent years. 'Entering the Promised Land' has been a theme in many sermons and songs; vision has been stirred and faith for the kingdom of God to advance, even for revival, has been growing. But still the city poses a challenge to us. At least in the West, most of the growth and renewal has taken place in suburbia and the provinces. Much as I rejoice in what has been happening, I remain convinced that any move of God which does not impact the cities will end up as superficial and domesticated – it will not be truly radical and it will not change the nations.

What has this renewal been for? It is not an end in itself, nor will tinkering with church structures satisfy us much longer. Already boredom is setting in – ask the teenagers in our churches. The growing commitment to evangelism, social concern and world mission are very healthy signs, but urban mission has not yet caught our imagination.

Inner city churches need renewal: celebration praise, an expectation of the miraculous, enlarged faith and vision. But renewed churches also need the inner city – to earth much that is rather ephemeral and as a testing ground. How do the things we have learned apply to less prosperous, more demanding front-line situations? If it is true biblically that the Holy Spirit comes to empower the powerless rather than the powerful, what might happen if those who have experienced His power were to invade the areas of powerlessness in our cities?

I long to see such an invasion taking place, and to see the walls of our fortress cities crumbling as God's Spirit works in great power. But I also fear the consequences unless we are prepared to seek humbly God's strategy for our cities. Joshua did not launch a frontal assault on Jericho, confident God would give him success. The first thing he did was to incapacitate his whole army by circumcising all the male Israelites; the second thing was to wait for God's strategy for taking the city.

The last thing the inner cities need is over-confident and triumphalistic Christians importing their ready-made solutions without any understanding of the local situation. The city has always represented human pride and self-sufficiency: if we go into the city with similar attitudes we risk becoming allies of the powers that enslave the city rather than deliverers. Praise and the confidence in God that flows from praise are vital elements in urban mission, as we shall see, but so is a servant heart and a humble recognition of our weakness in the face of the city and our need to know God's strategy for it.

The Prison City

Jericho was not just a fortress that kept the Israelites out: it was also a prison that kept its inhabitants in. We read,

> *'Jericho was tightly shut up because of the Israelites. No-one went out and no-one came in.'* (Joshua 6:1)

The walls which made the citizens feel secure also trapped them.

For many today the city feels like a prison; they feel trapped and powerless, overwhelmed by pressures but unable to escape. For many older people their tiny flats have become prisons; afraid to venture out they are trapped in loneliness and misery. Others, attracted to the city by its promises of freedom, excitement and opportunities, have become ensnared by its empty lifestyle. For others again the prison is economic, a vicious circle of unemployment, debt and depression.

If the Church is to minister to such needs, it must begin in the place Joshua found himself – flat on his face before God in worship and reverence. All kinds of solutions to the cities' problems have been put forward, almost all devised by those who do not live in the inner city where the problems are most acute. Perhaps if the architects who design housing estates were required to live there with their families, these estates might look less like the filing cabinets in the architects' offices and be more suitable for human occupation. It is vital the Church does not add more 'solutions' to an already confusing array, or else it will be met with the justifiable cynicism that greets the schemes of all outside 'experts'.

If we are to 'set the prisoners free', we need to discover God's strategy for the city we are concerned for. This brings us back, of course, to the strategies of prayer and prophecy that we have already examined. But it also leads us on to praise, for it was as Joshua worshipped the Lord that he understood how to approach Jericho. God often brings direction to His people as they worship Him. Celebrating God's wonderful deeds in the crossing of the Jordan imparted faith in the people so that they were not daunted by the city; worshipping the Lord gave Joshua the key he needed to unlock this prison city.

Joshua discovered three things as he worshipped the Lord. First, that he was on God's side rather than God being on his. This is the meaning of the enigmatic *'Neither'* (Joshua 5:14). The battle for Jericho was God's battle and Joshua was privileged to have a part in this. It was God who would take the initiative, God whose strategy would be adopted, God who would grant success. This is an important perspective for those involved in urban mission: the city often seems so big and overpowering – what can we do? But the city is God's problem, not ours. As our vision of God grows as we praise Him, we know that if He is at work in the city we can dare to be involved with Him there.

Second, the Lord tells Joshua that the city has been delivered into his hands (Joshua 6:2). Nothing outwardly had changed, the walls were still intact and the gates were tightly shut. But the outcome is no longer in doubt. The past tense is used and Joshua in faith receives this and tells the people to shout, because the city is now theirs (Joshua 6:16). To know that God's mission to the city will end in the victory of the New Jerusalem is a biblical and highly encouraging perspective on urban ministry. That is why having a theology of the city, which faces squarely its sin and rebellion but which looks ahead to the end of the story and sees the splendour of God's city, is so important.

Third, the Lord gives Joshua detailed and practical instructions about how to approach the city. It was not a normal strategy. To follow it risked looking very foolish if nothing happened when they shouted. It could only succeed if God acted miraculously. It was unique to Jericho – at the next city, Ai, Joshua was given a very different strategy. In urban mission too, cities are too different for pre-packaged solutions – evangelical, charismatic, denominational or any other sort. We need to wait on God for His strategy. He may ask us to do surprising things, very likely with a risk factor and a supernatural element involved, for nothing else will touch the supernatural forces at work in the city.

One of the greatest urban missions in history was launched in a gathering for praise and worship. Paul and Barnabas were set apart by the church at Antioch as the Holy Spirit spoke into this gathering.[1] Are we open for God to bring the challenge of the city into our gatherings for worship? Dare we engage in urban mission without being rooted in praise and worship?

The Power of Praise

Praise is not easy in the city. The physical environment does not form a natural backcloth to worship. The noise, rush and pressure of city life does not encourage adoration. Workmen digging up the road with pile-drivers on a Sunday morning is one of the many distractions the city can provide. And if we are right in seeing the cities as places of spiritual conflict, it is not surprising if there often seems to be a heavy atmosphere which hinders praise and worship.

But for urban churches praise is tremendously important: it is worth persevering with, worth the struggling to break through into the presence of God. The power of praise was a central feature of our teaching and experience during our twelve years in Tower Hamlets. We did not always live up to our ideals, but I remain convinced that praise and worship were crucial in our life together and in our witness.

A.W. Tozer describes worship as 'the missing jewel of the evangelical church'. I believe praise is the missing strategy in urban mission. Few books on urban mission give it any attention and none explores it in any depth. There are plenty of books around about praise and worship, but none that relate it to the city. But the connection needs to be made, for the current renewal in the praise dimension of the Church has rich potential for urban ministry.

Praise and worship focus us on God and provide an antidote to the secular urban environment. Whether we see the city as a fortress, a prison or as our home, praise enables us to look beyond it to the God who rules the whole earth. It is not that we are trying to escape urban realities; rather we are recognising another reality above and beyond the city which transforms the way we live in the city, equipping us to love it and bring words of hope to its inhabitants. Churches like the one I have been involved in are sometimes accused of escapism because of our emphasis on praise. If praise makes us detached from the city and insensitive to its needs, then it is selfish and escapist, but praise need not do this.[2] The ACUPA report indicates an alternative understanding of worship:

> 'Worship will put the harsh realities in a new light. It may enable people to withdraw for a time from the pressures, but it will be "withdrawal with intent to return", not evasion.'[3]

Our experience has been that meeting with the Lord, expressing our love and confidence in Him, rejoicing in His presence

and being refreshed in our spirits, has increased our commitment to our neighbourhood and renewed our strength to serve
Him there. Time and again God has spoken to us in the context
of worship, commissioning us afresh to witness and service in
the city. As we praise God and remind ourselves of His power
and love, the powers that seem to rule the city shrink in size and
fearfulness. We realise that they are *'weak and miserable principles'* (Galatians 4:9); we celebrate their defeat at Calvary; we
unmask them and see them under Jesus' feet. We realise that
they are still active, that we still face their influence each day,
but our perspective has changed.

Nothing about Jericho was changed when Joshua worshipped
the Lord, but Joshua was changed. As urban Christians worship
the Lord, we discover God's love for the city and are assured of
the ultimate success of His mission towards it. In praise we
bridge the gap between the 'already' and the 'not yet' of God's
kingdom. We rejoice in a victory that has already taken place
and we look forward to the consummation in the coming city of
God. Although present circumstances seem to contradict this
victory, we declare its truth and encourage each other to live in
the light of it. Praise is good for morale. The atmosphere of
gloom and discouragement that permeates the inner city can
easily infect the church. Small urban churches may easily feel
powerless and despondent; some of the books on the inner city
reflect this gloom – they are realistic in their assessment of the
problems but appear to have lost sight of the God of power and
joy.

Praise is not just for church meetings. It is a way of life, an
alternative to the grumbling and complaining that dominate
urban life. Listen to the conversations in any supermarket, bus
queue or launderette: the predominant feature is complaint.
Urban Christians (and others) can choose not to participate in
this but to use a radically different language of praise, thanks-
giving and contentment. A life of praise does not mean walking
around with a plastic grin, making trite comments; it does not
mean being insensitive to the pain and injustice in the city; it
does not mean stopping weeping or being angry about this.
What it means is that we live in an opposite spirit to that which
dominates the city. A lifestyle of praise declares our freedom

from the power of the city. It is an act of joyful defiance, a witness to both human and supernatural observers.

A praising community can be a very powerful witness. An Irish girl came into one of our meetings and was quickly in tears. As my wife talked with her, all this girl could say was 'God is here.' She listened to the message and was amazed to discover she could understand a sermon for the first time in her life, but it was the effect of the worship that brought her to Christ. Some time earlier a Hindu man from Mauritius was invited by a friend to one of our meetings. He was very quiet during the time of worship and at the end he explained why. He had seen a vision of Jesus on the cross with two other crosses in the background. He knew little about the Bible, so asked his friend if any others had been crucified with Jesus. When he heard about the two criminals he realised what he had seen and committed his life to Christ.

Praise is not just for church buildings either. In common with many other churches we took praise out on to the streets, marching around local markets and housing estates, singing, shouting, dancing and celebrating. There was a carnival atmosphere with children, balloons and clowns. The effect on the local community was remarkable. Traditional open-air preaching is ignored or produces a frown of disapproval, but these marches were greeted with smiles, clapping and genuine interest; even the heckling was good-natured. Door-to-door visiting in the area later confirmed the positive impact made by a joyful procession rather than a march of protest.

There has been quite a lot of teaching recently about praise as a weapon in spiritual warfare. The march around Jericho is one of several Old Testament passages used to illustrate this. The suggestion is that praise unsettles, binds or scatters the forces of darkness that oppose God's purposes. Praise marches are said to clear the atmosphere, push back the enemy and pull down spiritual strongholds. If this is so then urban Christians need to make use of this weapon against the powers in the city.

I do feel, however, that we must avoid unreality or going beyond what the Bible teaches. There is no New Testament teaching about praise as a weapon, and none of the Old Testament passages about praise actually say that praise is a weapon.

It is the setting for spiritual warfare, part of the preparation for it and the means of celebrating victories, but not a weapon itself. I am quite prepared to accept that the powers of darkness hate hearing God praised and feel uncomfortable where God's people are worshipping, but I suspect praise may actually have a greater effect on those who are praising than on the enemy.

Whether or not it functions as a weapon, praise is important for city churches. The dull, intellectual, repetitive worship of many churches in the past and still today not only did little to help the Christians express their love for God – it was positively off-putting to local people. In his booklet on urban church growth, Eddie Gibbs comments,

> 'more people are lost from the church through sheer boredom than from any other cause.'[4]

Praise and worship that involve the body and emotions, that invite participation, that avoid alien language, that do away with the one-man professional leader, are far more suitable for urban churches.

I believe too that the gift of tongues is particularly relevant in urban ministry. Many inner city people are afraid to pray aloud because they feel inarticulate and fear making mistakes. But the gift of tongues, according to Paul, bypasses the mind and operates through the spirit. Many urban Christians seem to receive this gift much more easily than mind-dominated middle-class Christians; as they become accustomed to it they experience tremendous release both in personal praise and in their ability to participate in corporate worship.

Joshua's success at Jericho was rooted in praise. As the people celebrated the ways in which God had worked at the Jordan, their morale rose and they were ready to shout in triumph; as Joshua worshipped the Lord he received the key to the conquest of the city. For urban Christians the goal is not the destruction of a city but salvation, renewal and release. This goal may seem distant at times, but as we praise God our hearts are stirred and we dare to take on our lips, perhaps at first in a whisper but eventually with a shout, the words of Joshua, *'The Lord has given you the city.'*

For Christians outside the city, especially those enjoying renewed freedom in praise and worship, the challenge of the city remains. How concerned are we to see the God we worship exalted in the city? Will our praising stir us to action – or will we be content just to sing songs about the Promised Land?

Chapter 12

Proclamation: Paul and the Cities of the Roman Empire

From City to City

'I believe that middle-class Christianity is the deviant form. Instead of the suburbanite trying to bring his Christianity to the city, it is about time we realised that the Christianity closest to the New Testament already exists in many store-front churches.'[1]

This provocative statement from American sociologist and author, Tony Campolo, is a reminder, as we consider various strategies to reach the cities, that urban churches have much to offer to others, as well as having needs to be met. The wider Church has much to learn from churches in the inner city, churches which are at the sharp end of mission, facing opportunities and difficulties that are beyond the experience of others.

It is important that urban churches are not patronised or seen just as poor relations. Many have a wide experience and incisive testimony; some have struggled with issues that many churches might regard as irrelevant to following Jesus because of the monochrome and prosperous surroundings in which they are working. Urban churches have struggled and failed but have also learned valuable lessons: their insights are needed by the wider Church.

We have already touched on some of these issues – power and powerlessness, gospel and culture, social justice and personal morality, evangelism and social concern. An obvious example of where inner city Christians have experience to share is their approach to racial diversity. There have been various models, mistakes and misunderstandings: some urban churches are all-white; some are all-black; some are predominantly white but have happily welcomed into their fellowship brothers and sisters from other ethnic backgrounds; some are truly multiracial, culturally sensitive and demonstrating the unity of the Spirit in a way that transcends racial barriers. In our own church we enjoyed some wonderful 'mixed marriages', including one with a Turkish Cypriot groom, a Columbian bride and a Portuguese best man!

Many churches outside the city have little awareness of such issues; some would regard them as of marginal significance; not a few demonstrate racist attitudes themselves – on occasions this has been blatant and offensive, more often it is expressed in patronising arrogance and cultural superiority. Living and witnessing in the inner city gives Christians a different perspective on a range of issues from those based in the suburbs. These perspectives are not always right, but they need to be heeded. I believe urban churches have a prophetic role not only towards their cities but also towards the wider Church, challenging its complacency, identification with the successful and powerful, and insensitivity towards human needs.

In the early years of the Church, it was Jerusalem that was the 'mother church', that represented stability and orthodoxy, where large numbers of Christians lived. They had experienced the power of the Spirit in remarkable ways, they were led by godly and experienced leaders, their fellowship was exemplary. But it was from Antioch that the Roman Empire was evangelised; at Antioch the disciples were first called 'Christians' (Acts 11:26); in this pagan, cosmopolitan city the gospel was proclaimed to Gentiles as a matter of policy (Acts 11:20); from here Paul and Barnabas were commissioned to spread the gospel throughout the cities of the Empire (Acts 13:1–2).

The leaders of the church in Jerusalem agreed in principle with these developments. Discussing the unexpected conversion of the Gentile Cornelius, they concluded, *'God has granted even the Gentiles repentance unto life'* (Acts 11:18). But the word 'even' indicates their surprise and there seems to have been no practical outworking of this discovery. It was in Antioch that theory became practice. Radical advance took place not in the Christian heartland but on the frontier of its mission. It had taken persecution to get the church moving from Jerusalem, but the church at Antioch was outward-looking from its inception. Its membership was culturally and racially mixed (as was its leadership) and there was a readiness to act radically and generously, giving away both financially (Acts 11:27–30) and their best leaders.

The church at Jerusalem got wind of these exciting but rather unsettling developments and sent Barnabas to investigate. His openness was a tremendous encouragement to the young church at Antioch, as was his bold decision to draw in Paul who was still too hot for the Jerusalem church to handle. It is to the credit of the Jerusalem church that they rejoiced to see what was happening, even though Peter and others later still found it hard to handle (Galatians 2:11–13).

The church at Antioch needed the encouragement and affirmation of the church in Jerusalem, but the assistance was not all one way. Urban churches today need the help of the wider Church, but they also have a contribution to make. Will they be given an opportunity to make it? Will their concerns be written off as unimportant to the advance of God's kingdom, or will there be those as large-hearted as Barnabas, willing to listen? Many inner city churches have a rough and ready feel to them; they tend to be less organised, more informal, less literate, a little raw, exciting but disturbing and not always congenial to middle-class Christians. They have their faults and weaknesses, but they also have important strengths. There is potential for ministry from the city as well as to the city.

Good News for the City

Sent out from Antioch, Paul and his companions travelled from city to city across the Empire (Acts 16:4). There is no evidence that Paul ever evangelised villages: his goal was to plant in each city a church that could then take responsibility for the evangelisation of the surrounding area.[2] He did not do what most

Christians today do – avoid the cities because of their sinfulness, poor environment or pressures. Nor did he neglect the poor in these cities. Although he debated with philosophers and could count nobles among his converts, he had a special concern for the poor (Galatians 2:10).

What was the good news that he proclaimed in the cities? Many books have been written about the message that the Early Church preached, but there are still a number of points that are relevant to contemporary urban mission.

First, it was *good* news that was proclaimed. Paul was not ashamed of his message. He did not regard it as an imposition on his listeners, but as an exciting, dynamic and life-changing word. He knew that God was good and gracious and he spoke words of hope and encouragement in the cities. There is so much bad news in the city, so many pressures and problems, so much that weighs people down and makes them miserable. Jesus said that He had come to bring *good* news to the poor and oppressed (Luke 4:18). The city needs good news. The sort of preaching that loads condemnation on people, that increases their sense of failure and worthlessness is not helpful – far too much open-air preaching smacks of this. Paul preached at Lystra about the goodness, kindness and abundant provision of God and told them, *'we are bringing you good news'* (Acts 14:15–17). Proclaiming good news to the city means discovering how to bring good news to the 'sinned against' as well as to 'sinners'.

Second, the call for repentance was clear and specific. Paul confronted the superstitious idolatry in Lystra and urged the citizens to *'turn from these worthless things to the living God'* (Acts 14:15). The good news is only good for those who repent: we can have no excuse for playing this down or failing to speak about the lordship of Christ.

> 'Urban evangelism has had more than its share of "easy decisions" and it has left the city unchanged and unimpressed.'[3]

Some have so emphasised the oppression of the poor that they have failed to preach repentance. The urban poor are certainly the victims of oppression and have been sinned against, but they are also sinners like all men and women and need to repent. A diluted gospel actually further degrades and penalises people. It is not good news to be told that you are merely the victim of circumstances, environment and upbringing; it is great news that, in spite of these very real factors, you are still responsible for your life, able to repent and free to start again under the leadership of Christ.

Third, the call to repentance was phrased in a way that could be understood. Paul spoke about what he could see the citizens of Lystra doing, rather than about sin as a concept. Urban mission requires us to abandon 'conceptual' ways of talking and use a more 'concrete' approach. It also requires us to assume no knowledge of the Bible or theology on the part of our hearers, to avoid Christian jargon, and to earth timeless truths in very contemporary media. Compare Paul's messages to the Jews, who had a biblical heritage, and the Gentiles who did not: in the former there are many references to the Scriptures, in the latter there are none, but Paul does quote from a pagan author.[4]

Fourth, the good news was actually proclaimed – it was not just lived out but preached, argued, explained, discussed and communicated in every possible way. Many urban churches (and others) have lost their nerve here, afraid of offending people. They have found various ways to justify their existence without proclaiming the gospel: a policy of maintaining the existing flock and sacred building; substituting social concern for evangelism; adopting a 'remnant theology' to explain the falling numbers; concentrating on children's work; political involvement about issues alien to local people. Many of these options they justify theologically, but I suspect most are simply due to loss of nerve – what East Londoners would refer to as having 'no bottle'. This attitude is defeatist, suicidal (the closure rate of such churches is alarming) and not justified historically. As in biblical times, the response to the gospel has been mixed in the cities, but many have responded. And, as Paul asks, *'how can they hear without someone preaching to them?'* (Romans 10:14) – if there is no proclamation, nobody will respond. I am convinced there is a greater openness to the gospel in the inner cities than elsewhere: it is time we overcame our reticence and recovered our evangelistic nerve.

Fifth, the uniqueness of Jesus was proclaimed without compromise. In Athens Paul was distressed by the city's idolatry; in Lystra he made this his starting point. The loss of nerve in evangelism is particularly evident in this area. In multi-faith urban areas many churches are very wary of speaking clearly about Jesus as the only way to God. We were criticised by local church leaders for proclaiming the gospel to Muslims. Some suggested that to do this is a form of fascism or cultural imperialism, adding to the difficulties the community faces. Our response was that to avoid this community (perhaps 40,000 in Tower Hamlets) and to fail to share with them the greatest news ever would in itself be racist. We recognise the need for sensitivity, but we will not compromise on the uniqueness and centrality of Jesus. Paul lived in a multi-faith society. His insistence that Jesus alone was Lord was no more congenial to his society than to ours, but it happens still to be the truth.

There is no way of avoiding the fact that the main New Testament urban strategy is evangelism. Presence, prayer, praise and prophecy played their part, and the proclamation was supported by works of power, which we will look at next, but communication of good news was central to urban mission. I suspect, furthermore, that evangelism is particularly relevant in the inner city, bringing good news to the poor, and that prophecy will be mainly directed towards the rich and powerful in the city centres, calling them to account for the state of the cities they control, bringing what may at first sound like bad news, but which carries within it a call to repentance that will result in freedom for both oppressor and oppressed.

Evangelism in the City

So much then for Paul's message. How did he present it in the cities of the Empire? What were his methods? The New Testament does not provide a blueprint, nor is urban evangelism essentially different from evangelism elsewhere. Perhaps the most important factor is the diversity within the cities and the demanding task of finding appropriate ways to communicate the gospel. Rigid, systematic approaches are not the answer: however much they may claim to be biblical, they inevitably carry a good deal of cultural baggage with them. We have used a wide range of approaches with varying degrees of effectiveness. We have no easy answers, so all this section will attempt to do is to look briefly at some familiar forms of evangelism and their likely impact on the city.

(1) Visitation

Many urban churches have followed Paul's example (Acts 20:20) and visited people in their own homes – to invite them to meetings, to give them literature, to pray for the sick, to offer practical help, or simply to explain the gospel on the doorstep. Some urban missioners have rejected this approach, either because it seemed ineffective or because it was felt to be inappropriate. Ray Bakke argues that urban people suffer from 'psychological overload' due to the high number of casual relationships in urban life, and he asks,

> 'What do you suppose then is the effect of door-to-door calling upon strangers? Very low. People live in locked buildings because they do not want any more casual relationships.'[5]

Having done a lot of such visitation over the past decade I sympathise with this assessment, but I am not convinced that door-to-door visiting should be abandoned. One of the advantages of visiting in the inner city is that most people are blunt enough to let you know very soon if they are not interested, rather than politely wasting your time. This enables visitors to concentrate on those who welcome a visit, and in our experience there are many who do. Our cities are full of lonely, sometimes desperate people, feeling imprisoned in their homes; for some a visit from a caring person, even a total stranger, may be a tremendous encouragement. Provided we are prepared for a long-term approach I believe that visitation offers many opportunities for proclamation and a caring ministry.

I accept that using natural contacts with family, friends, workmates and neighbours is preferable, but we have found that when church members are mobilised for visitation they become much more ready to use these natural contacts as well.

In any case, the tiny percentage of Christians in many inner city areas means that without calling on strangers it is hard to see how most people can be reached at all. A further advantage of visitation is that it is a demonstration that the church realises it has no reason to expect people to come to its buildings and meetings; it fulfils the Great Commission to 'go' rather than waiting and hoping.

(2) Open-air Outreach

This form of proclamation has clear biblical precedent and many historical examples (see Acts 14:8–18; 17:17; 19:30–31 etc). We have touched on it in earlier sections, but it is worth underlining the need for creativity, joy and sensitivity here. Open-air outreach need not be drab and dour, nor need it be verbal only. Both the content and presentation need to take into account who will be watching and for how long. Short personal testimonies, the use of colourful costumes, music and dance, mime and juggling, banners and street theatre can communicate so much more effectively and winsomely than lengthy incomprehensible sermons.

William Booth, the founder of the Salvation Army, is reputed on one occasion to have been carried into Whitechapel market in a coffin by four bearers in traditional attire, who stopped and put the coffin on the ground. When a curious crowd had gathered, Booth flung open the lid and emerged to preach about the resurrection. The only reason we have not tried the same method has been the difficulty of obtaining a coffin – and a slight concern lest anyone watching should suffer from a weak heart!

Open-air witness can also contain a prophetic element. When Christians from various social and racial backgrounds stand together, this in itself points to the reconciling power of the gospel; the joy and celebration expose the gloom and pressure of urban life. Effective open-air witness defies the powers and presents an alternative for the city.

(3) Literature

If literature is to be used in urban mission, we really need to think radically about what to use. The vast majority of evangelistic literature available today is unsuitable: it is designed for a middle-class culture, uses Christian jargon, uses far too many words, assumes too much and attempts to go too far too quickly. We also need to realise that over ninety per cent of the literature we use goes straight into the bin, so expensive high-quality leaflets are bad stewardship.

Just as the New Testament, the evangelistic literature of the Early Church (once it had been written and circulated), was written not in sophisticated Greek, but in the common speech of the day, so we need to produce literature that is suitable for urban people. Bearing in mind the need for flexibility, it is often best for local churches to produce their own, rather than relying on mass-produced glossier alternatives. We can learn a lot, if we are willing to, from the broadsheets distributed by local political groups and commercial advertisers.

(4) Meetings

Since there is no biblical example of church-based evangelistic meetings, it is surprising that these form the main part of many churches' evangelistic programme. When Paul wanted to arrange a public meeting, he hired a secular hall (Acts 19:9). There may be compelling reasons to use a church building, but normally we use them more for our own convenience than for the comfort of those we hope to invite – many of whom in the inner city find church premises alien and threatening. Public halls, homes, pubs and community centres are 'neutral territory' – we had many more accept invitations to our 'Tankard 'N' Testimony' evenings in a local pub than would come to our Sunday meetings.

Roy Joslin suggests that evangelism via church buildings is not only ineffective but unjust:

> 'Generally speaking the working man is not willing to go to church – it is outside his circle; he does not belong to that class. But if we make the main focus of our evangelism the preaching of the gospel from the pulpit, we are discriminating unfairly against the working man.'[6]

However we use meetings, we dare not equate unwillingness to come to church buildings with rejection of the gospel. The great majority of those we saw converted became Christians outside of church meetings – and some have still struggled to come into our buildings after this.

(5) Missions

What effect do large-scale missions have on the city? The use of neutral venues such as football stadia, high-profile publicity and the mobilisation of local churches all promise much; and the New Testament refers to Paul's work on occasions arousing city-wide interest (Acts 13:44; 17:8; 19:10, 29). The evidence suggests, however, that inner cities are hardly affected by such ventures.

Often the publicity projects a very middle-class image (the Mission to London in 1984 was a classic example of this, with Luis Palau in a businessman's suit); the distance involved to get to the venue is often beyond what inner city people are willing to consider; and such missions are most effective among those on the fringes of the church, rather than among the unchurched masses in the inner cities. Any inner city people who do attend – such as a couple I took in 1984 – are embarrassed at being expected to sing Christian songs they do not know, and the appeals for finance (there were three that evening) confirm the suspicion that the Church is just after their money.

Lessons have been learned and the 1989 Mission England was much more sensitively handled, but far more radical changes are needed if these missions are to touch the inner cities. Until then, they will be useful for the suburban churches with their large fringes of nominal churchgoers, and exciting for mission groupies who occupy the front row every evening, but they will have a marginal effect on urban mission. The most inner city churches can hope for is to gather up the crumbs by making use of the event as a conversation starter in local outreach.

There is no doubt that urban churches, like most others, grow mainly as a result of ordinary Christians gossiping the gospel to friends and neighbours; all the above methods are secondary to this. The church in Antioch was founded by unknown people, as were those in most cities of the Empire, including Rome itself. The key to urban mission is not new methods or a new message, but the mobilisation of ordinary believers. By all means let us examine the evangelistic possibilites and make them as sharp and relevant as we can, but in the end we are back again with the primary need in urban mission – the increased presence of ordinary Christians, working, worshipping, living and witnessing in the city.

Church-planting in the City

Paul's ministry in the cities did not stop at proclamation. His constant practice was to plant churches where his converts could be nurtured and discipled (Acts 14:21–23). Church-planting has not been in vogue for some time in Britain. It has been assumed that the nation has enough churches, and that the emphasis should be on the renewal and expansion of these. But church-planting is vital, not least in the inner city where hundreds of new churches, and new **kinds** of churches, are needed to fill the huge gaps that exist. It has been very encouraging to see signs that this subject is back on the agenda, and to recognise that the closure of urban churches is not the only trend of the past few years – the planting and growth of new churches in the inner city is also taking place.

Some still argue that working within established structures to revive existing churches is the better way. Several have urged this in seminars on church-planting I have led. I am glad whenever this happens but, as someone has commented, 'having babies is easier than raising the dead.' Planting new churches, where new foundations can be laid and the traditions and trappings of the past need not hinder present mission, is often a more effective use of limited resources. Where there is openness to renewal and change it may be worth persevering, but often it is like hitting one's head against a brick wall. Some struggling churches need to close down, in spite of the sentimental pressure to stay open, so that the true state of urban mission can become clear and new initiatives emerge.

It is not an either-or situation. Even if significant renewal and growth were to take place in every inner city church in the nation, there would still be room for more churches. Until every local community unit (often the housing estate) in the city has a viable Christian community worshipping and witnessing in it, there is room for church-planting.

Such a strategy involves more than evangelism. Many would define it as an apostolic ministry. The term 'apostle' is used more widely today than for many years, but where are the *urban* apostles we need to initiate and mobilise resources for this church-planting programme? The restoration of the apostolic ministry will not be achieved by calling men apostles who are functioning as non-denominational bishops, nor by planting new churches to compete with others in suburbia. The avoidance so far of the urban challenge demonstrates that we have some way to go until we recover the apostolic ministry of Paul who could write:

> '*It has always been my ambition to preach the gospel where Christ was not known, so that I would not be building on someone else's foundation.*' (Romans 15:20)

But church-planting is back on the agenda, all over the world, even in established church circles, where the inadequacy of the parish system in urban mission is being recognised, and this promises much for the future of mission in our inner cities. Urban churches are crucial for the proclamation of the gospel in our cities. The evangelist is no more called to be a loner than the prophet. Both need to be able to say with integrity and confidence, 'Come and see what I am talking about.' The local church is where urban people will judge whether the good news works or not. They may not come to church meetings or church buildings at first, but if they discover the life of Jesus in Christians they meet, the church is fulfilling its calling to be a 'city set on a hill', giving light to all around. It is a visual aid, a working model of all the evangelist is proclaiming.

> 'As the world becomes increasingly urban, with city populations mushrooming everywhere, we must learn what it means to advance the gospel among city people and plant among them living churches, lighthouses of the kingdom of the Lord Jesus Christ.'[7]

Chapter 13

Power: Philip and Samaria

'Those who had been scattered preached the word wherever they went. Philip went down to a city in Samaria and proclaimed the Christ there. When the crowds heard Philip and saw the miraculous signs he did, they all paid close attention to what he said. With shrieks, evil spirits came out of many, and many paralytics and cripples were healed. So there was great joy in that city.'   (Acts 8:4–8)

In Word and Deed

It really did not seem fair. Persecution had successfully broken up the burgeoning church in Jerusalem and scattered the disciples all over the place. Saul was doing a great job in tracking down the believers and hauling them off to prison. Satan's plans seemed to be bearing fruit. But once again the tables were turned and his worst assaults were used by the Holy Spirit for the advance of God's kingdom. Instead of hiding away, the scattered believers were proclaiming Jesus everywhere. The good news was no longer confined to one city; it had broken out and was spreading like wildfire over all Judaea and Samaria. Before long it would reach Antioch and then the whole Empire would be affected.

Luke concentrates on just one of these believers, Philip, one of the seven who had been appointed to serve at the tables. There is no way of telling whether Luke chose his ministry as a typical example of what was happening or whether it had unusual features, but one can imagine Satan wishing he had left

Philip serving at table where he was doing less harm. The result of his ministry in Samaria is the result that all who are involved in urban mission long for – *'great joy in that city'* (Acts 8:8). There is much unhappiness in the city, loneliness, sickness, frustration and pain: how crucial is the release of the power of God that can bring joy!

Philip, like Jesus before him and Paul later, combined *proclamation* with *demonstration* of the good news. When the crowds saw his miracles of healing and deliverance, not surprisingly they *'paid close attention to what he said'* (Acts 8:6). His deeds of power won him a hearing, authenticating his message. Even the local sorcerer was impressed and became a follower, recognising a greater power than he could summon up (Acts 8:13).

Evangelism in both word and deed was normal in the New Testament. Jesus was acknowledged as *'powerful in word and deed'* (Luke 24:19); he told John's companions to report *'what you hear and see'* (Matthew 11:4) – the healing of the sick, the raising of the dead and the preaching of good news to the poor. Although he refused to perform miracles for the sceptical, he urged doubters to weigh carefully the meaning of his miracles:

> *'even though you do not believe me, believe the miracles, that you may know and understand that the Father is in me, and I am in the Father.'*   (John 10:38)

Signs and wonders do not automatically convince people or lead to their conversion. The reaction may be hostile or indifferent. At times proclamation alone may suffice. But demonstration does make an impact, confronting people with the presence of God's advancing kingdom. The narrative in Acts makes it clear that evangelism in word and deed was not restricted to Jesus but was the practice of the Early Church and one of the keys to the growth of the church. Nor was it restricted to the apostles, as some have suggested. We could easily have used Paul as a focus for this section,[1] but Philip was an ordinary believer doing extraordinary things in the power of the Spirit. The cities need apostles, but they also need ordinary believers demonstrating the good news they are proclaiming.

In many parts of the world today biblical evangelism is being restored and explosive church growth is taking place. Even in the materialistic and intellectual West, a 'paradigm shift' is taking place and there is a new expectancy of signs and wonders. If we can avoid the two dangers – of claiming too much and inviting disillusionment, and of internalising these things instead of using them in evangelism – we could be on the brink of a similar advance.

Power in the City

The restoration of biblical evangelism is important for churches everywhere, but once again I believe there are factors that make it particularly significant in urban mission.

First, the absence of the natural world. Paul writes:

> *'For since the creation of the world God's invisible qualities – his eternal power and divine nature – have been clearly seen, being understood from what has been made, so that men are without excuse.'* (Romans 1:20)

He is not saying that observing the natural world leads to saving faith, but that there is no excuse for ignoring the testimony of the natural world to God. City-dwellers, though, may feel that they *do* have an excuse. Living in a man-made environment, protected from all but the most severe weather conditions, where even the stars that caused the Psalmist to reflect on God and humanity are obscured by urban haze, where is the evidence of God?

Occasional trips to the countryside do not fill the gap – indeed many inner city friends we have taken out to the country have found it a hostile and unpleasant place; they have been glad to return to the warmth and familiarity of the city. But urban people need to discover the power of God: if the natural world does not do this for them, we need to be open to alternatives. We may not accept that city-dwellers have a valid excuse for ignoring God just because of where they live (there are other signs, such as conscience), but it is important we take seriously their need to be confronted by the power of God. Signs and wonders may meet this need: they will not automatically convince, but they do break into the complacency and secularism of the city.

Second, the experience of powerlessness. We have referred to this before, as have many Christian and secular writers. Decisions are taken elsewhere, problems seem insoluble, change seems unlikely and people feel insignificant. We will consider later the Church's call to identify with this powerlessness, but part of the answer is power. It is a tremendous thing for urban people to discover that God is powerful and able to intervene in their lives; that He answers prayer and transforms circumstances that oppress; that God rather than the Housing Department has the final word on where they live; that God can change the hearts of hostile neighbours; that God can break through the barriers of fear and sickness that cripple people. This is good news urban people can respond to.

Third, the prevalence of illness and oppression. The inner city is not a healthy place. Statistical evidence indicates that life expectancy is lower than in suburbia;[2] there is a lot of disease and disability. Atmospheric pollution, the pressure of urban life and the various effects of poverty all contribute to this.[3] Waiting lists for medical treatment are long, private care is out of the question. Despite contrary claims Government cuts always affect the poor most seriously. The healing power of God is needed in our cities, both to demonstrate the good news and to meet the huge physical and emotional needs of urban people.

Fourth, the pragmatism of city people. Much of our evangelism attempts to answer the question 'Is it true?' – persuading people that the Bible is reliable, that the resurrection was historical, that Christianity is logical. This is valid but it is not what most city people are interested in. The question of truth cannot ultimately be dodged, but the pressing issue is, 'Does it work?' If it works, there is a good chance it may be true, but if it does not work, what does it matter whether it is true or not?

It was the miracles that gained Philip a hearing. Effective urban ministry must include demonstration. Our experience of this is limited and we long for much more, but what we have seen has convinced us that this is vital. The period when we saw most people converted coincided with the time when we were most conscious of the power of God, healing the sick and setting free the demonised. For several months people were coming to Christ at a rate of four a week. Most of them had either experienced the power of God in their own lives or had seen its effect on others. Without exception, every convert from another religion (Muslim, Sikh or Hindu) came to Christ as a result of a power encounter of some kind.

As in the New Testament, we have found that not all who are touched by the power of God come to faith in Christ. One memorable example was when a member of our church prayed for a Muslim man who was very ill with diabetes and about to be hospitalised. The man was healed and came to our meeting on the next Sunday to say through an interpreter, 'Your Jesus has healed me.' To the best of my knowledge his diabetes has not returned, but neither has he become a Christian.

But many have found Christ through their encounter with the power of God. Some already knew about the good news but had not responded before; others knew practically nothing but the power of God opened their hearts to the gospel. I believe there is a hunger for God in urban areas that will lead to a huge harvest being gathered in once the Church discovers how to tap into the power of God. Words alone are not enough.

Fifth, conflict with the powers. Philip's ministry is set in the context of conflict – the opposition of Simon the sorcerer and the institutional oppression that had scattered the Church. It had been the miracles done in Jerusalem that had so threatened the powers in that city, but Philip's response is to continue evangelising in word and deed. The city, as we saw in an earlier chapter, is the headquarters of demonic opposition to the rule of God. Urban mission involves a power encounter. Whether it is confronted by awkward individuals, institutional antagonism or supernatural opposition, the Church in the city needs the power of God. It must be able to pray with authority, to stand firm in the strength of God, and to minister in the power of the Spirit.

I am not convinced we have a mandate to 'bind the powers' in any blanket sense, as some have tried to do (they still seem remarkably unbound to me); but we are to discern where the powers are at work, so that by prayer and action we can counter their influence. If the Church in the city is to fulfil God's intention that *'through the church, the manifold wisdom of God should be made known to the rulers and authorities in the heavenly realms'* (Ephesians 3:10), it must be present in strength, prophetic in lifestyle, clear in proclamation, joyful in praise and powerful in deed. Such a church has the potential to make a real difference to the city.

Hope in the City

But how much difference can the Church make? Unrealistic hopes are at least as damaging as despondency. The ultimate hope for the city is in the New Jerusalem coming down from heaven. Promising more than we can deliver will not endear the Church to inner city communities already used to the broken promises of planners and politicians. But the response to Philip in Samaria, and to Paul in Ephesus, gives us hope that the power of God can radically affect our cities.

We have considered several reasons why the recovery of the power of God is of special significance for urban mission. Is there any reason to hope that this power *will* be experienced in a fresh way in the cities? I believe there is. God seems to delight in doing the unexpected and humbling the pride of men and women. The inner city may be just the place where God chooses to act in great power and bring genuine revival. Jesus' miracles were often in the context of preaching the good news to the poor.

Furthermore, the inner cities are pioneer mission situations. Michael Green writes:

> 'In missionary areas, where there is only a tiny church in a vast pagan stronghold, where there is a shortage of medical means, where there may be no translations of the Scriptures available or where the people are as yet illiterate, where, furthermore, there are definite spiritual lessons to be reinforced by it – there, on the fringes of the gospel outreach, we have a situation in which we may expect to see God at work in miraculous ways today.'[4]

It is clear from the context that he is thinking of non-western primitive societies, but what he has written applies also to urban mission in the West. Here too the Church is tiny and in a pagan stronghold; medical means may be available but the long waiting lists are damaging people's health – healing by miracle is becoming increasingly necessary; the effectiveness of literature is small, with little available still for some ethnic groups; and, as we have seen, there are definite spiritual lessons to be learned from the experience of God's power.

Not all would agree that the ministry of power is as restricted to frontier situations as this quotation suggests, but if Michael Green is right, urban churches can expect to be among those which experience the power of God in their ministry. If Sodom and Tyre would have responded to a ministry of miracles, as Jesus assures us they would (Matthew 11:21–22), there may yet be hope for our cities when the power of God is released through His people.

The Power of the Powerless

Exercising a ministry of power is one response to the powerlessness that pervades the inner city, but it is not the only one. Indeed power – especially spiritual power – is fraught with danger if not set into the right context. That context is a willingness to identify with the powerless in the city. To be voluntarily powerless is another way of resisting the power of the city, another example of living in an opposite spirit to all that the city represents.

Jesus was at the same time the most powerful and the most powerless person who ever lived. He was the Son of God who could have called on a legion of angels at any time. He was filled with the Holy Spirit to such an extent that on occasions power had *'gone out from him'* to heal (Mark 5:30). He spoke with such authority that crowds were awed and the soldiers who came to arrest Him fell to the ground when He spoke (John 18:6). But He was also powerless. He had no settled home during His years of ministry. He had no human power base – economic, political or military. He refused to use violence and forbade His followers to fight. He had no money of His own but depended on the charity of others. He spent His time with the

131

common people, the outcasts and the disreputable. He refused to endorse the status quo and was provocatively antagonistic towards the establishment. He was killed as a threat to social stability, and His death was a clear demonstration of His powerlessness, a pitiful figure on a cross.

Those who would follow Jesus do not have the right to pick and choose which parts of His life to copy: we are to imitate both His powerless stance and His powerful ministry. Both aspects of His life have been emphasised by different groups in recent years, but as yet they are rarely brought together. Charismatics have been thrilled by the discovery that the power of Jesus is still at work through the Church. Radical evangelicals, Liberation theologians and others have rejected civil religion, protested against the conformism and middle-class ethos of the Church and looked for ways to live more like Jesus in solidarity with the poor and powerless. For many this has meant choosing to live in the inner city rather than the comfortable suburbs.

Urban churches (and others) need to take on board both aspects of Jesus' life. The Early Church had no human power or status, nor did it seek these, but the power of God enabled it to turn the Roman Empire upside down. Philip ministered in the power of the Spirit but he had no other influence or power. It was the power of these powerless disciples that so baffled and upset the authorities in Jerusalem:

> *'When they saw the courage of Peter and John and realised that they were unschooled, ordinary men, they were astonished and they took note that these men had been with Jesus. But since they could see the man who had been healed standing there with them, there was nothing they could say.'*
> (Acts 4:13–14)

Urban churches do not need international superstars to bring ministries of power to the city – unless they identify with the powerless. Such ministries may be exciting and touch individuals, but the message they convey is once again that solutions are not to be found in the inner city, so experts have to be imported. This confirms the sense of powerlessness and further discourages local initiatives. What is needed is someone with an experience of the power of God who will come to serve and equip: it was this attitude that made the visit of one of John Wimber's teams such an encouragement to our church. The danger of ministries of power is, if they do not challenge the injustices and demonstrate sensitivity to the issues that confront urban people, that they may 'more and more powerfully reinforce the status quo'[5] – in the long run playing into the hands of the powers in the city.

The Church in the city needs to explore ways to identify with the powerless. This will require radical changes, for at present it is widely regarded as part of the establishment. It will involve looking at issues we have mentioned already – the financing of urban mission and the use of church buildings. It also means a fresh approach to the development of leadership in the churches.

Paul and his companions, when they had established a church in a city, did not import trained and qualified leaders to run it. Sometimes a member of the team was left behind for a while (for example, Titus in Crete), but his or her primary task was to appoint local elders. The leadership of the churches was placed in the hands of local people. Although Paul counsels against the appointment of a recent convert, this must have been a relative term (see Acts 14:21–23). There is certainly no suggestion in the new Testament that academic qualifications, social responsibility or formal training are required of church leaders. The main requirements were to do with personal integrity, family stability, local reputation and spiritual gifting.

The way in which most church leaders are appointed means that the odds are stacked against urban Christians. They often do not have the academic background, the financial support or the inclination to go through the training process. Those that do are often ruined by it and ineffective when they return to their local patch, if they ever return at all. 'A way should be made for the recognition of the ministries of non-academic working-class people,' writes Michael Armitage from Brixton. They should not be 'forced to cope with middle-class obstacle races in order to be ordained but encouraged to explore and develop their own great gifts.'[6]

Men and women of spiritual maturity and ability are wasted

by such a procedure. The emergence of local urban church leaders is vital if the church in the city is to be earthed and identified with the powerless. Nothing that we have said earlier about the relocation of Christians into the city should obscure this. The continued importing of professional church leaders reinforces the dependence of city churches; those who come in must come to serve rather than to dominate.

Church buildings, ecclesiastical wealth, professional clergy and the identification of the Church with the establishment all invaded the Church in the three or four centuries after the death of its first-generation leaders, culminating in the unholy alliance of Church and State under Constantine. The powerlessness of the Church disappeared – as did its power. It was no longer turning the world upside down. It had become the bastion of the status quo. From a persecuted Church it had become a persecuting Church. The Church had conquered the Empire – or had it been absorbed and domesticated by it?

An early pope said to a visitor to Rome, 'no longer can St Peter say, *"Silver and gold have I none."'* His visitor replied, 'True, but nor can he say now, *"In the name of Jesus, rise up and walk!"'* The ministry of power continued in the Church well after the first generation. Many later writers refer to miracles and healings. Augustine mentions several examples in his day. But the power was ebbing away. The Church's refusal to be powerless went hand in hand with its loss of power. It lost both its radical stance and its charismatic dynamism. The urgent task of the Church today is to recover not one but both.

Chapter 14

Patience: John and the New Jerusalem

'I am coming soon. Hold on to what you have, so that no-one will take your crown. Him who overcomes I will make a pillar in the temple of my God. Never again will he leave it. I will write on him the name of my God and the name of the city of my God, the new Jerusalem, which is coming down out of heaven from my God; and I will also write on him my new name.'   (Revelation 3:11–12)

Letters to Urban Churches

One of Satan's greatest coups has been to get the Church squabbling about the final book of the Bible. He has a vested interest in this, for it is here that his final ignominious defeat is made clear. His great alternative to God's purpose, Babylon the Great, has been devastated and in its place the glorious New Jerusalem descends from heaven. Instead of arguing about the significance of every detail, or ignoring the book because it seems so obscure, we need to reclaim it for what it is – a tremendous message of encouragement to seven city churches facing persecution and internal difficulties. Each church receives a specific letter, but all seven are shown the amazing future that God has planned for His people, if only they will patiently endure until the Lord comes.

The task of urban mission will not be accomplished over-night. It will not be achieved by hit and run missions, by church leaders 'doing a stint' in the inner city before moving out to more prosperous and congenial parishes, or by groups that spring up suddenly and die equally quickly, like the plant which sheltered Jonah as he waited for God to zap Nineveh (Jonah 4:5–7). Rapid growth, exciting developments, even revival have their place in urban ministry, but so does patient endurance.

Urban people are not impressed by those who come charging in with bright ideas and grand schemes. The normal reaction is, 'give him a year or two and he'll be off.' Cynical perhaps, but based on experience and often correct. The turnover of all kinds of professionals in the inner city is enormous. Teachers and social workers are forever moving on. One can sympathise with the North Philadelphia woman who, served by nine separate city welfare departments and their rapidly changing staff threatened to shoot the next social worker who came to her door.[1]

Church leaders tend to last a little longer but few stay long-term. David Sheppard writes:

'There has been an unspoken career structure for the ordained ministry; it is fine to go to the inner city or housing estates when you're young, strong and free, but, if you're any good, you should then move on to minister to a "more thoughtful" congregation. Then when you are old, you go to a rural parish. Urban and rural areas both suffer from this. The strong churches receive much more than their share of what are judged as the most able and mature ministries.'[2]

Let me emphasise again that I am not denying that God may sometimes call people out of the city into suburban or rural areas, either temporarily or permanently. My concern is with the small number of church leaders (and members) who are prepared either to move in or to stay in, serving God patiently in the city. It takes as long as many stay simply to become culturally tuned in and able to communicate. Just when they are accepted and ready to make an impact, they are off, further endorsing the analysis of local people.

Writing to the seven city churches, John introduces himself to them as *'your brother and companion in the suffering and kingdom and patient endurance that are ours in Jesus.'* (Revelation

1:9). These three aspects of our life in Jesus are all important in urban mission.

There is a cost involved. Urban mission is not easy; church life in the inner city can be discouraging; raising families there has both advantages and disadvantages. Some suffering is unnecessary, caused more by foolish strategies than anything else. One of the most obvious needs is to abolish one-man ministry situations. Team leadership is the clear New Testament pattern: in the context of the inner city, one-man ministry is foolish in the extreme and has led to nervous breakdowns, resignations, even suicide. The appointment of single leaders, rather than teams, to lead city churches is short-sighted, wasteful and cruel; this is an area that urgently requires fresh thinking by denominational boards and mission groups.

But not all suffering is unnecessary, however unaccustomed we may be to including this element in our inheritance in Christ. I hope by now I have made clear my conviction that the inner city is one of the most exciting and rewarding places a Christian can be. Many of the fears and prejudices that hinder us from considering it are groundless. Serving Christ at the sharp end in urban mission is challenging and demanding, but it does seem closer to New Testament discipleship than the more comfortable version we often replace this with. Nevertheless there is a price to pay.

The churches to which John wrote were facing various problems. Some were undergoing outright persecution, which had already claimed the life of one church leader (Revelation 2:13), and which would lead to imprisonment and possible execution for others (Revelation 2:10). Others were plagued by false teaching – some had spotted and rejected this (Revelation 2:2–6), but others had been deceived and were going astray (Revelation 2:14–15). In some immorality and compromise with paganism were blighting their witness (Revelation 2:20); in another it was the creeping disease of lukewarmness that threatened the church (Revelation 3:15–16).

John does not offer an easy way out. Instead he invites the churches to step back and see the grand scheme of God's purposes. The second reality he reminds them of is 'the kingdom'. It is clear from the teaching of Jesus that this kingdom is both present and future. It has come and is yet to come. The new age of the Spirit has broken into the present age through the death and resurrection of Jesus, but the present age has not come to an end. The powers, including the power behind the city, have been conquered, disarmed and exposed, but they are still at large. The Church is called to live and witness in this overlapping of the two ages. Its task is to show the world what God's tomorrow will be like. Fulfilling this calling in the cities is one of its main responsibilities, because of what the city represents – the rejection of God's plans and the attempt of human beings to build their own tomorrow. In spite of the suffering involved, the church in the city is to proclaim the good news of the kingdom that is coming and has already arrived.

The link between suffering and the kingdom is the third reality John mentions. Patient endurance is one of the main themes of the book. The phrase 'him who overcomes' which is repeated many times can be translated 'him who endures to the end'. Victory in the New Testament is not triumphalism. It is the ability to stand firm patiently. Deceived by the attitude of modern society, which expects quick returns and instant answers, we are eager for something to show for our work. Patient endurance is not a popular subject. The New Testament does encourage us to expect growth and fruitfulness, but it also calls us to be patient, both as we wait for the return of Christ to establish the kingdom and as we continue to proclaim the good news of the kingdom.

There is work to be done; there are opportunities for service. In Philadelphia the church is told of a wide open door (Revelation 3:8) – the church may feel weak and weary, as many urban churches do, but the day of opportunity is still present. The reward for faithful service is a share in the coming city of God. If we want a share in that city, we have work to do in ours.

John gives the churches a wonderful vision of the risen Jesus, walking among the lampstands that represent the churches. More than anything else they needed to see Jesus enthroned over their cities and moving among them. The book begins with a vision of Jesus and ends with a vision of the New Jerusalem. The city of God is still future, a hope which inspires urban mission and enables us to endure, but Jesus is already enthroned and at work. In Him the kingdom has already arrived. City churches, like all others, are living in the in-between time, testifying to the kingdom of God and praying for its consummation.

An Unfinishable Task

Just as the building of the city is always in progress and never completed, so urban mission will continue until Jesus returns. None of the churches Paul established now exist. In each generation the challenge of the city faces the Church afresh – not least in our generation as cities explode all over the world in unprecedented growth. To acknowledge that the task is unfinished is not to admit defeat. Realising that the entire human race will not be converted does not stop us preaching the gospel. Much can be achieved, but not everything. Real change can take place, but not Utopia. There is hope for our cities, but Babylon will still emerge and be destroyed before New Jerusalem replaces it and the job really is finished.

It is in this context that we need to consider a number of verses which speak about flight from the cities. Isaiah and Jeremiah both counsel flight in certain circumstances,[3] as later Jesus did. Can it then be argued that Christians should not remain in the city? The Bible speaks so clearly of the city as a rebellious institution, a focal point for demonic power, a place where sin is concentrated and judgement is imminent. In Revelation the call to leave the cities is endorsed:

> *'Come out of her, my people, so that you will not share in her sins, so that you will not receive any of her plagues.'*
> (Revelation 18:4)

Perhaps the trend away from the cities is right after all? Are Christians who choose to live in the city putting themselves and their families at risk, exposing themselves to a sinful society and the danger of being caught up in judgement when it falls? This is the position Lot was in when the angels warned him to flee the city.

The Bible is clear that flight from the city is a proper strategy in certain circumstances, but there are a number of qualifications to this.

First, flight is only to be contemplated when the voice of God is heard calling His people out. He may speak in various ways, but it is His voice we need to listen to. There are many other voices with persuasive reasons for abandoning the cities, but what is God saying?

Second, in most of the Old Testament references there is a purpose to the flight. It is not just leaving Babylon that is at stake but returning to Jerusalem to rebuild that city. The exiles were called out of one city into another. Similarly, when Jesus speaks about flight it is only as far as the next city:

> *'When you are persecuted in one place, flee to another. I tell you the truth, you will not finish going through the cities of Israel before the Son of Man comes.'*   (Matthew 10:23)

The task, says Jesus, is unfinishable and at times flight will be necessary, but the cities still wait for us to return to them.

Third, each time the call to flee is sounded it is an indication that judgement is imminent. Lot and his family just escaped in time. Babylon had reached the point of no return and was about to fall. Jeremiah had earlier urged the exiles to settle down in the city, but now flight was the best strategy. Only when there is no hope left is this so, and even then the attitude of those leaving is not 'good riddance' but sorrow:

> *'We would have healed Babylon, but she cannot be healed; let us leave her and each go to his own land, for her judgement reaches to the skies.'*   (Jeremiah 51:9)

Jesus told His disciples:

> *'When you see Jerusalem surrounded by armies, you will know that its desolation is near. Then let those who are in Judea flee to the mountains, let those in the city get out and let those in the country not enter the city. For this is the time of punishment in fulfilment of all that has been written.'*
>
> (Luke 21:20–22)

Once again the call to flee is in the context of imminent judgement. The disciples are not to leave at once, for there is much work to do in spite of the difficulties there, but they are to be watchful and detached enough to flee at the right time. Two ancient writers, Eusebius and Epiphanius, record that just before the Roman army laid siege to Jerusalem prior to its destruction, the church recalled this warning, left the city and fled to Pella across the Jordan, so escaping the carnage.

Fourth, when the Old Testament passage about flight from the city is quoted in the New Testament, the emphasis is not upon geographical separation but moral. Paul tells the church in Corinth, a city notorious for vice and degeneracy,

> *'come out from them and be separate, says the Lord.'*
> (2 Corinthians 6:17, quoting Isaiah 52:11)

The church is to be separate *within* the city, so that its witness is effective. It is not to be ensnared by the spirit of the city, but normally this does not involve leaving the city itself.

Our conclusion is that on occasion flight is the right strategy, but it is only when all else has failed and when the voice of God is clearly heard. When the call to flee comes, there must be no delay, for we are citizens of another city and *'here we have no lasting city'* (Hebrews 13:14 RSV), but we are not to anticipate this call. When the call comes it will be because our continued presence in the city would be meaningless and would achieve nothing, but until then there is work to do.

The New Jerusalem is our goal and destiny. There will be a day when we will all hear the call to leave the urban nightmare that our city has become, which Babylon the Great represents, to go to another city, unlike all others, where we will at last be at home. But until then the task of urban mission remains and the quality that must mark our ministry is patience. It is this that must undergird all the other strategies we have explored. We are involved in a mission that cannot be completed by men and women but to which God will write the final chapter. What we can do is to work towards that vision and make a difference in our cities and in our generation.

141

'We are on a pilgrimage of faith and will not see the ultimate accomplished nor the city of God erected here by our efforts. By man's own doing, or even by the vigorous efforts of Christian men and women, cities of earth can never become the city of God we seek ... But still the pilgrimage continues, attracting impassioned men who share the dream of the heroes listed in Hebrews, a vision of the city of God, the world at the feet of Jesus.'[4]

Chapter 15

Putting It All Together:
Nehemiah and Jerusalem

If any book in the Bible can be described as a manual for urban ministry, it is the story of Nehemiah. Written almost in the form of a diary, it recounts not only the way in which the ruined city of Jerusalem was restored and repopulated but also the inner struggles, joys and concerns of the man himself. We have only touched on Nehemiah's ministry in earlier chapters, but in this final chapter we will use his story to draw together the threads and to underline what is of special importance. It may be also that we will catch a little of his passion, for without this all the strategies we have looked at will be lifeless.

Jerusalem lay in ruins. Many years had passed since Nebuchadnezzar had devastated it, some of the exiles had returned and there was some attempt at community life. But life was tough, resources were scarce and an air of despondency hung over the city. Far away in imperial Susa, Nehemiah had not forgotten Jerusalem; when some visitors from there arrived he questioned them eagerly about what was happening there. Their answer broke his heart:

> *'Those who survived the exile and are back in the province are in great trouble and disgrace. The wall of Jerusalem is broken down, and its gates have been burned with fire.'*
>
> (Nehemiah 1:3)

The starting point for Nehemiah was concern for the city and a longing to see the situation changed: it is no different today

143

for those who would serve God in the city. Our task is not to rebuild a physical city, but just as ancient Jerusalem was not an end in itself but a sign of the coming City of God, so our work in the city – which has spiritual, social and physical dimensions – is a pointer to that City. There are many lessons to be learnt from Nehemiah.

Prayerful Concern (Nehemiah 1:4–2:9)

For four months Nehemiah sought God for the city, fasting, weeping and praying. We are told no more about this formative period, but out of it came the prayer that is recorded here. By now Nehemiah had discovered God's perspective on Jerusalem; he had studied the Scriptures and heard the Lord calling him to get involved. His main concern now is that his employer – who happened to be the emperor – would release him to go to Jerusalem.

Praying for the city is dangerous! God is looking for those who will share His concern for it, and those who pray may find themselves called to be part of the answer to their prayers. As for Nehemiah, this may involve radical changes in lifestyle, employment, security and location. But Nehemiah had heard the voice of God, he had identified with the needs of the city, and he was confident that God would act to change the situation. It was this period of prayer that was the foundation for his ministry. Prayer is the first strategy in urban mission.

By the time Nehemiah took his life in his hands and asked for permission to go to Jerusalem, his vision and purpose were clear. The emperor's response was a great encouragement – not only was he allowed to go but he was given building materials, letters of authority and an armed guard. Not many urban missioners will be given such equipment, but we can share Nehemiah's experience of knowing that *'the gracious hand of my God was upon me'* (Nehemiah 2:8). It is this assurance, born in prayer, that can sustain us however discouraging the circumstances may be.

Thorough Preparation (Nehemiah 2:10–21)

Three days after his arrival in Jerusalem, Nehemiah began to prepare for the task that lay ahead. First, he made a thorough inspection of the walls to see for himself what needed to be done. He did this at night so as not to draw attention to himself, but he was left under no illusions about the size of the project he was committed to. At one point there was so much rubble he had to dismount and complete his inspection on foot.

Second, he encountered the opposition, led by Sanballat the Horonite. He and his friends were disturbed and offended by the arrival of Nehemiah and accused him of false motives and empire-building. As soon as his intentions became known he was mocked and ridiculed. These men would be a hindrance throughout his ministry, so it was as well for him to meet them now and resist them firmly at the outset. He declared his mission, announced his confidence in God and challenged their right to influence in the city.

Third, he assessed the work-force. However strong his sense of calling, he could do little alone. The success of his mission depended on willing volunteers. He had a list in his mind of who would be doing the work – even the priests and nobles would be asked to join in – but he said nothing until he had understood the situation.

There are lessons here for any contemplating urban ministry. Rushing in with preconceived ideas will lead to trouble; it will be inappropriate to the local situation, it will alienate local people and it will risk being vulnerable to enemy activity. Humility, discernment and patient preparation are needed. The trust of local people needs to be won and their hopes rekindled: they may have lived with ruined walls for a long time. Clever strategies which have 'worked' elsewhere have a conspicuous lack of success in the inner city. And the cost of urban mission needs to be counted: the city is a centre of opposition to the purposes of God. Time spent listening, looking and learning will not be wasted.

When we have done this we are ready to declare to the powers that dominate the city what Nehemiah said to Sanballat:

> *'you have no share in Jerusalem or any claim or historic right to it.'* (Nehemiah 2:20)

They have usurped the city, but they have no right to it. We are not prepared to share it with them, but in the name of Christ we have come to rebuild and restore. Careful preparation and bold declaration are not incompatible.

Effective Mobilisation (Nehemiah 3:1–32)

A chapter full of unpronounceable names! We may be tempted to pass over this as of no contemporary relevance. But this is the work-force, an army of ordinary people, each doing his or her bit (for women played their part too in what was traditionally a male job – see v. 12). They had caught Nehemiah's vision and were prepared to work to see it realised.

The rediscovery of the priesthood and prophethood of all believers has been of great importance in recent years, but it needs to be carefully guarded. Laziness, disorganisation, professionalism and a clergy-disguised-as-elders can soon creep back into churches which have preached and practised 'body ministry'. In urban churches particularly there is a strong temptation to let the obviously able or articulate members carry responsibility and do the significant jobs, but this will not in the long run be the most effective way. Those who come to serve God in the city are coming to encourage local Christians, not to take their place or do everything for them. There is often a need for outside stimulus, to renew vision and initiate action, but those who follow through this strategy of increasing the presence of God's people in the city must not ride rough-shod over those already there.

It is so easy to feel insignificant in a large city. What difference can one person make? This list of names may be dull to us because we know none of the people mentioned, but it assures us that the ministry of each individual is recorded in heaven – even the attitudes of the workers are noted (vv. 5, 20). Effective mobilisation of urban Christians will require us to find ways to honour and convey significance to their ministries, to counter the powerlessness and inadequacy so many experience.

A careful reading of this section also reveals that two types of work were necessary – repairing and rebuilding. In some places the wall was not totally destroyed; it was damaged but still standing. But elsewhere there were gaping holes. The same is true in urban mission – in some places the church is weak but

146

alive and in need of strengthening and renewal; in other places there is rubble to be cleared away (unhelpful traditions, crumbling and useless buildings) and huge gaps where there is no real church life at all. In these areas pioneering and church-planting are needed.

Serious Opposition (Nehemiah 4:1–23; 6:1–19)

Sanballat and his cronies tried everything they could think of to discourage the workers, to distract them, to intimidate and stir up antagonism against them, to destroy their unity and their reputation. Although they pretended to pour scorn on the rebuilding, they were really furious and greatly alarmed, aware of the significance of what was taking place. Nehemiah was kept busy resisting these attacks, exposing their schemes and reassuring the people, some of whom were finding the going tough. His threefold strategy was prayer (Nehemiah 4:9), praise (Nehemiah 4:14) and persistence (Nehemiah 4:17). Whatever the opposition, the rebuilding continued.

Urban mission involves conflict. I have heard much about spiritual warfare and how to live victoriously, but quite honestly I have found much of it rather tame and nebulous. Opposition in the city is often blatant, sustained and unpleasant – it is not a little annoyance that is attributed to the devil 'having a go'. We ourselves or friends in the inner city have been variously vilified in the local press, pursued with a shotgun, chased with a kitchen knife, threatened by a letter written in blood and disturbed every hour of the night with hostile phone calls. I mention these incidents partly to help those who are considering urban ministry to be realistic, and partly to plead with Christians elsewhere to stop trivialising spiritual warfare.

One of the temptations in situations of conflict is to spend all our time fighting and to lose sight of our main purpose. Nehemiah maintained a careful balance here, his workers having a weapon in one hand and a tool in the other. The real victory was not frightening off the enemy but completing the wall. We eventually read the thrilling words:

> *'So the wall was completed on the twenty-fifth of Elul, in*
> *fifty-two days. When all our enemies heard about this, all the*

> *surrounding nations were afraid and lost their self-confidence, because they realised that this work had been done with the help of our God.'*   (Nehemiah 6:15–16)

At the end of the day Satan is not too worried by our praise marches: but he hates to see churches planted and the people of God increasing in numbers, influence and holiness in the city.

'There is something exciting about urban mission,' writes Roger Greenway. 'Just because it is so difficult, when the breakthroughs occur and renewal comes, God's grace will be shown in unmatched splendour.'[1] When revival comes to the inner city it will be evident that this is God at work. Those who live in the suburbs are generally successful in many areas – why not in their churches also? But in the inner city, where success is not the norm, where problems are complex and people feel inadequate, if God acts in power there is no other way of explaining it.

The conflict may be great but that is because the stakes are high. Satan knows it, and it is time the Church realised it too and put its resources into the front line where the battle is fierce but the potential for significant advance is great. The cities are crucial – and most surprisingly to our way of thinking the inner city is the key to the city.

Integrity and Justice (Nehemiah 5:1–19)

It was not just external opposition that Nehemiah faced; there were internal problems too, bad feeling and division that were hindering the work on the wall. The main cause of this was a debt problem. Many poor Israelites had been forced to borrow money to pay the imperial taxes and to mortgage their homes to buy enough to eat. There had been famine in the land and the poverty-stricken citizens of Jerusalem could not make ends meet without going into debt. When they were unable to pay what they owed their children were taken into slavery. The cry of the people was, *'we are powerless'* (v. 5).

Debt is still a major problem in urban areas (as elsewhere). Some are in debt because of unwise purchases or dishonesty, but many more have simply not been able to make their income match their basic expenditure. The availability of credit, its attractive packaging and persuasive advertising have lured people into this modern form of slavery. The extortionate rates of interest charged make escape from the debt trap very difficult.

The Church's lack of involvement in urban areas may incline it to respond harshly or judgementally to this situation – blaming those who are in debt. But the credit companies and others who charge high interest rates must shoulder some responsibility for what has happened, as must those responsible for government policies that have encouraged such activities. The Church has an opportunity here, as in various other areas, to side with the oppressed or the oppressors, to be seen as the bastion of an unjust establishment or as a defender of the poor. Compassion, debt-counselling and practical help, together with prophetic and political action to deal with root causes could make a significant difference.

Nehemiah was angry but he thought carefully about the way forward before approaching the creditors. Accusing them of oppression and extortion, he urged them to declare an amnesty and to return indebted property to its owners. The only way out of the mess was for those with power to show mercy and to put right past injustices: the transactions may have been legal but they were not just.

But if the Church is to speak or take action it must demonstrate integrity itself. Nehemiah had moral authority in the city because he had not participated in these injustices. He had chosen to live simply, to forgo privileges and to show generosity. His motivation was both to please God and to avoid laying any more burdens on those who were already weighed down. If the Church is perceived as wealthy and seen spending lots of money on its own buildings and projects and always asking for money, it will not be trusted by the poor and the powerless. Unfortunately that is the very image the Church has in many inner city communities, an image that will not be changed without radical action. But that is the cost of developing a strategy of prophecy.

Joyful Celebration (Nehemiah 8:1–18; 12:27–47)

The wall was finished. In spite of all the difficulties it had taken a mere fifty-two days, an amazing achievement which thrilled the builders and dismayed their opponents. The disgrace and despair were replaced by joy and celebration. Just as the power of God at work in Samaria would bring great joy in that city, here in Jerusalem they rejoiced as they realised that the hand of God was upon them.

Two celebrations are recorded. The first was a huge public meeting in the city, which began with praise and worship, continued with a public reading of God's word for several hours, and concluded with great feasting and celebration. The Levites explained to those unfamiliar with the Scriptures what it all meant – just as urban churches must find ways to interpret the Bible to those who find its language confusing.

The immediate response of the people, when they realised how far short they fell of God's law, was to weep. Such a response was right and a quarter of the following day was spent in public confession, but the leaders encouraged them first to rejoice. They had had years of misery and now the wall was built: it was a day for celebration. *'The joy of the Lord is your strength,'* explained Nehemiah (Nehemiah 8:10). As we have seen, praise and joyful celebration are so important in the city, banishing discouragement and fear, renewing the morale and strength of the people.

Jesus in Nazareth quoted from Isaiah about releasing the oppressed, binding up the broken-hearted and proclaiming good news to the poor. The passage goes on:

> *'to comfort all who mourn in ... Zion – to bestow on them a crown of beauty instead of ashes, the oil of gladness instead of mourning and a garment of praise instead of a spirit of despair ... They will rebuild the ancient ruins, and restore the places long devastated; they will **renew the ruined cities** that have been devastated for generations.'* (Isaiah 61:2–4)

Good news for the poor needs to be proclaimed in the city; praise, joy and celebration are vital. This need not result in sin being excused or the radical demands of Christ being watered down, but it will enable those already very aware of failure to respond with hope.

The second celebration was the occasion of the dedication of the wall. Two huge choirs were assembled, musicians were appointed and an enormous praise march around the city took place. When Joshua marched round the walls of a city it was with the faith they would shortly collapse; the celebration here was a triumphal procession that the walls their enemies said could not support a fox jumping on them were solid enough for the people to march on. Praise in the city is a testimony to the triumph of Jesus through His death and resurrection over the hostile powers of the city, a denial of their rule and a declaration of confidence among God's people. It is also a tremendous witness:

> 'The sound of rejoicing in Jerusalem could be heard far away.'   (Nehemiah 12:43)

Tithing People (Nehemiah 10:37–11:2)

One result of reading the law was the recovery of the practice of tithing that had been abandoned. The leaders went a step further than tithing their goods, however: they

> 'cast lots to bring one out of every ten to live in Jerusalem.'
> (Nehemiah 11:1)

The re-population of the city was achieved by a mixture of personal volunteering and corporate strategy: some were commended for choosing to live in the city, others were conscripted from the various surrounding towns and villages. The tithing of people was one way of meeting the needs of the city.

Tithing is an Old Testament practice. Although not abolished in the New, it is not endorsed by the Early Church and Jesus, though He does not condemn it, certainly warns against the legalism that can accompany it. Only the Pharisees are recorded as practising it, in spite of the fact that very full teaching about giving is provided. The restoration of tithing in many churches today may be sound financial policy but it is based on dubious biblical foundations; in churches which have emphasised grace and freedom the requirements of tithes is a strange anomaly. The New Testament clearly urges regular, proportionate and generous giving, but it strongly encourages us to leave the amount to the conscience of each individual. Jesus' teaching and Early Church practice indicates a much more radical approach to finance than tithing, drawing on the Jubilee teaching of the Old Testament.

Some churches commit themselves to giving away at least a tenth of their income to avoid being selfish and parochial. Perhaps some would consider urban mission as a valid recipient of such giving (though bearing in mind the dangers outlined earlier where outside finance is concerned). Any church that begins to catch a glimpse of God's purposes in the city will want to find some practical way of expressing its concern.

The conscripting of people to move into the cities is no more acceptable today than the requirement of tithing, but as with finance it is an interesting and provocative illustration. As well as commending volunteers who choose to get involved in urban areas, rather than discouraging them as some do, could not a flourishing suburban or provincial congregation be challenged to consider the possibility that God might want several of them to move? The diagram in chapter 2 might help explain why so radical a strategy is worth considering. Ray Bakke says,

'I now include in my lectures on Nehemiah an appeal to people to move into one of Chicago's scarcely habitable districts, and some do respond ... This sounds like a radical strategy, but it is as old as Nehemiah.'[2]

An Unfinished Task (Nehemiah 13:1–31)

The glorious praise march would have been a fitting climax to Nehemiah's ministry – and an upbeat way of ending this book. But honesty compels Nehemiah to add another section to his diary, in which it is clear that ongoing ministry is needed. While Nehemiah was away, reporting back to the emperor, things started to go wrong – one of his opponents was allowed into the temple, the tithes were not collected, the sabbath was misused and dangerous intermarriage with pagans was taking place.

Nehemiah could justifiably have been discouraged when he returned. What had his ministry achieved if his reforms had so quickly been set aside? But his response was to deal firmly and decisively with the problems. Tobiah's furniture is thrown out of the temple on to the street, various officials are sacked, and his promise to 'lay hands on' sabbath-breaking traders has very different connotations from its New Testament usage! His treatment of those who had intermarried is not to be found in most pastoral manuals either:

> *'I rebuked them and called curses down on them. I beat some of the men and pulled out their hair.'*
>
> (Nehemiah 13:25)

Whatever we may think of his methods, his passion and determination are clear. A degree of ruggedness, but blended with compassion, is needed in urban ministry.

One final glimpse of Nehemiah finds him making provision for the wood and firstfruits for the temple ceremonies, a mundane anticlimax after the celebrations of the previous chapter. But the Bible is always realistic. God's mission to the city is unfinished. Jerusalem was a sign of the coming City of God, but no more than this. We can do much in our cities as we await this City, but only Jesus can bring this work to conclusion. In the meantime we are to get on with the daily tasks of urban ministry.

The story of Nehemiah is an account of just one man. His arrival in the city and his godly ministry there made a crucial difference to Jerusalem in his generation. We read earlier that the absence of just 'one man' in Jeremiah's day led to the destruction of the city. Nehemiah was prepared to be the one person in his day who took to heart the plight of the city, saw the opportunity and acted.

Cities today seem so overwhelming; the inner city seems so alien. But God is still looking for individuals who will 'stand in the gap' with Him and share His urban mission. His heart still goes out towards the cosmopolitan megacities that present the greatest challenge to the Church at the end of the second millennium.

Notes

Chapter 1

1. Nathanael in John 1:46.
2. The 1991 English Churches Census, as reported in *'Christian' England* by Peter Brierley.
3. Harvie Conn estimated in 1983 that only 8.6% of evangelicals were in cities of 1 million or more. See *A Clarified Vision for Urban Mission*, p. 17.
4. Roger Greenway, *Apostles to the City*, pp. 26–7.
5. See, for example, the account of Die Innere Mission in Germany in Craig Ellison, ed. *The Urban Mission*, p. 31; and various accounts in Robert Linthicum, *Empowering the Poor*.
6. This approach has been lauded by some and criticised by others – see Daniel Callaghan, ed. *The Secular City Debate*. A more recent volume by Harvey Cox, *Religion in the Secular City*, qualifies the views expressed in the original book.
7. Richard Farnell, ed. *Powerlessness and the Inner City*, p. 18.
8. *Faith in the City*, ACUPA para 3.44.
9. Raymond Bakke, *The Urban Christian*, p. 23.

Chapter 2

1. Quoted by Roy Joslin in *Urban Harvest*, p. 48.
2. *Ibid.*, p. 46.
3. Bakke, *op. cit., p. 102*.
4. Harvie Conn in *A Clarified Vision for Urban Mission*, pp. 27–9.
5. With apologies to Luke 18:9–13.
6. Quoted by Ron Elsdon in *Bent World*. IVP 1981, p. 75. For similar American studies, see Conn in *A Clarified Vision for Urban Mission*, pp. 72–4.

Chapter 3

1. 1 John 5:19.
2. Harvie Conn in *Discipling the City*, p. 227.
3. See, for example, Ezekiel 27:4–11.
4. See Jeremiah 6:6; Ezekiel 22:6–13; Amos 4:1 etc.
5. See Nahum 1:14; Micah 5:11–14; and cf. Acts 17:16; 19:34.
6. See also Habakkuk 2:12; Jeremiah 26:15; Ezekiel 22:3–4 etc.
7. See also Ezekiel 22:6–13; Nahum 3:4 etc.
8. See also Ezekiel 16:49; Isaiah 3:9; Ezekiel 27:3; 28:2 etc.
9. See Isaiah 26:1–6; 60:14–18; 62:12; 65:17–25; Zechariah 2:4–5; 8:3–5; Ezekiel 48:35.
10. Ellul, *op. cit.*, p. 88.
11. See Psalms 46, 48, 87, 122, 125, 127, 132.
12. See, for example, Zephaniah 3:1; Ezekiel 22:3; Amos 6:8; Ezekiel 16.
13. See, for example, Isaiah 1:21–26; Jeremiah 33:8–9.

Chapter 4

1. Job 1:7.
2. Revelation 18:2.
3. Psalm 55:11.
4. David Sheppard, *Built as a City*, p. 430.
5. Matthew 28:18.
6. Galatians 4:9.

Chapter 5

1. Winston Crawley in *An Urban World*, ed. Larry Rose and Kirk Hadaway, p. 38.
2. Matthew 5:14.
3. See, for example, Matthew 21:43.

Chapter 6

1. Acts 2:12.
2. See also Joel 3:1–2; 11–12; Jeremiah 3:17; Micah 4:2.
3. See also Acts 13:44; 21:30.
4. Revelation 21:26.
5. Revelation 19:1.
6. Revelation 18:22–23.
7. Revelation 18:10, 17, 19.
8. See Chapter 3.
9. Revelation 22:1–2.
10. Luther Copeland in *Discipling the City*, p. 70.

Chapter 7

1. Conn in *A Clarified Vision for Urban Mission*, p. 15.
2. Jock Stein in *Ministry and Mission in the City*, p. 8.
3. Roger Greenway in Greenway and Monsma, *Cities Missions' New Frontier*, p. 45.
4. Benjamin Tonna in *Gospel for the Cities*, p. 89.
5. Winston Crawley in *An Urban World*, p. 40.
6. Bakke in *The Urban Challenge*, ed. Rose and Hadaway, p. 119.

Chapter 8

1. Ray Bakke, *op. cit.*, p. 65.
2. cf. *Christian Witness to the Urban Poor*, p. 6: 'The church as a whole is trapped in ignorance about the urban poor, the causes and consequences of poverty, and the extent and gravity of our complicity in it.'
3. A useful manual on this subject is *Preparing for Battle* by Peter Adams, for a while a member of our church. This was published jointly by YWAM and Kingsway in 1987.
4. Roger Greenway in *Apostles to the City*, p. 40.
5. Dave Cave in *Jesus is Your Best Mate*, p. 100.

Chapter 9

1. Psalm 137 ends, *'O Daughter of Babylon, doomed to destruction, happy is he who repays you for what you have done to us – he who seizes your infants and dashes them against the rocks.'*
2. Eddie Gibbs, *Urban Church Growth*, p. 22.

Chapter 10

1. See, for example, Isaiah 17; Jeremiah 49; Ezekiel 29–30; Amos 1; Zephaniah 2.
2. Reported in IDEA, magazine of the Evangelical Alliance.
3. The Christian Schools Movement has both advocates and opponents, but several urban leaders have reorganised the potential of Christian schools in inner city ministries. See, for example: Donald Benedict, quoted in *Urban Ministry*, p. 194; John Perkins in *With Justice for All*, p. 184. Regal Books, 1982.

Chapter 11

1. Acts 13:1–3.
2. Eddie Gibbs (*op. cit.* pp. 7–10), drawing on evidence from South America, pleads for a style of worship that is relevant to the life-situation of the congregation and the local community. He

emphasises the need for participation, the expectancy of meeting with God and the renewal of commitment to society that such worship can result in.

3. ACUPA, para 6.108.
4. Gibbs, *op. cit.*, p. 7.

Chapter 12

1. Quoted in *Starting All Over Again* by John Vincent, p. 54. WCC 1981.
2. See, for example: Robert Brow, quoted in *Discipling the City*, p. 108; Michael Green, *Evangelism in the Early Church*, pp. 317–18. Hodder and Stoughton, 1970.
3. Roger Greenway in *Apostles in the City*, p. 81.
4. Acts 13:16–41; cf. Acts 17:22–31.
5. Bakke, *op. cit.*, p. 59.
6. Joslin, *op. cit.*, p. 91.
7. Greenway, in *Apostles to the City*, p. 13.

Chapter 13

1. See Acts 14:3, 8–10; 16:16–18; 19:11–20.
2. See, for example, Erlich, *Population, Resources and Environment*, p. 179.
3. For more details, see Elsdon, *op. cit.*, pp. 69–70.
4. Green, *op. cit.*, p. 233.
5. A comment made by Walfred Fahrer, a Mennonite pastor.
6. Michael Armitage in *Jesus Loves Brixton Too*, p. 102.

Chapter 14

1. Quoted in Elsdon, *op. cit.*, p. 72.
2. Sheppard, *op. cit.*, p. 373.
3. See Isaiah 48:20; 52:11; Jeremiah 50:8; 51:6, 9, 45.
4. Greenway in *Apostles to the City*, p. 13.

Chapter 15

1. Greenway in *Discipling the Cities*, p. 95.
2. Bakke, *op. cit.*, p. 73.

Further Reading

A. Stories of Inner City Church Life

Jesus is Your Best Mate, Dave Cave. Marshall Pickering, 1985.
Jesus Loves Brixton Too, Michael Aritage. Marshall Pickering, 1986.
Rivers in a Dry Land, Eddie Neale. MARC, 1989.
Ten Inner City Churches, ed. Michael Eastman. MARC, 1988.
Youth in the City, Peter Stow. Hodder and Stoughton, 1987.

B. Books About Urban Life

Built as a City, David Sheppard. Hodder and Stoughton, 1974.
City of God?, Nicholas Bradbury. SPCK, 1989.
Signs in the City, Colin Marchant. Hodder and Stoughton, 1983.
The Urban Christian, Ray Bakke. MARC, 1987.
Urban Harvest, Roy Joslin. Evangelical Press, 1982.

C. Theological/Philosophical Reflections on the City

Powerlessness and the Inner City, ed. Richard Farnell. Shaftesbury
    Project, 1981.
Religion in the Secular City, Harvey Cox. Simon and Schuster, 1984.
The Meaning of the City, Jacques Ellul. Eerdmans, 1972.
The Secular City, Harvey Cox. MacMillan Co., 1965.
The Secular City Debate, ed. Daniel Callaghan. MacMillan Co., 1966.

D. Strategies for Urban Mission and Ministry

A Clarified Vision for Urban Mission, Harvie Conn. Zondervan,
    1987.
An Urban World, ed. Larry Rose and Kirk Hadaway. Broadman
    Press, 1984.

Further Reading

Apostles to the City, Roger Greenway. Presbyterian Reformed Publishing Co., 1973.

Christian Witness to Large Cities, LCWE 1980, Paper 9.

Christian Witness to the Urban Poor, LCWE 1980, Paper 22.

Cities Missions' New Frontiers, ed. Roger Greenway and Timothy Monsma. Baker, 1989.

Discipling the City, ed. Roger Greenway. Baker, 1979.

Empowering the Poor, Robert Linthicum. MARC, 1991.

Faith in the City. Church House, 1985.

Gospel for the Cities, Benjamin Tonna. Orbis Books, 1982.

Guidlines for Urban Church Planting, Roger Greenway. Baker, 1976.

In the Inner City, Greg Smith. The Handsel Press, 1987.

Into the City, John Vincebt. Epworth Press, 1982.

Ministry and Mission in the City, Jock Stein. Handsel Press, 1987.

Taking Our Cities for God, John Dawson. Word, 1989.

The Responsible Suburban Church, Gaylord Noyce. Westminster Press, 1970.

The Urban Challenge, Larry Rose and Kirk Hadaway. Broadman Press, 1982.

Urban Church Growth, Eddie Gibbs. Grove Books, 1977.

Urban Ministry, David Claerbaut. Zondervan, 1983.